*Kevin C. Fitzpatrick*

# 111 Places in the Bronx That You Must Not Miss

*Photographs by Joe Conzo Jr.*

emons:

To the memory of my grandfather,
FF Joseph Fitzpatrick,
Hook & Ladder Co. 137, FDNY.
– K. C. F.


For my moms.
– J. C.

© Emons Verlag GmbH
All rights reserved
© Photographs: Joe Conzo, except:
Henry Hudson Monument (ch. 45): Alex Rivera, www.thebronxer.com;
Kingsbridge Armory (ch. 55): Alex Rivera;
New York Botanical Garden (ch. 106): Michele Gouveia;
Wave Hill (ch. 107): Alex Rivera
Art Credits:
Big Pun Mural (ch. 14): TATS Cru;
Wall Works (ch. 105): John CRASH Matos
© Cover motif: Wilfredo BIO Feliciano, TATS Cru
Edited by Karen E. Seiger
Layout: Eva Kraskes, based on a design
by Lübbeke | Naumann | Thoben
Maps: altancicek.design, www.altancicek.de
Basic cartographical information from Openstreetmap,
© OpenStreetMap-Mitwirkende, ODbL
Printing and binding: Lensing Druck GmbH & Co. KG,
Feldbachacker 16, 44149 Dortmund
Printed in Germany 2019
ISBN 978-3-7408-0492-3
First edition

*Did you enjoy this guidebook? Would you like to see more?*
Join us in uncovering new places around the world on:
www.111places.com

# Foreword

One cold morning, three guys stood in the Riverdale woods, staring down at a drone. We were ready to launch it towards heaven when a big, friendly, slobbering dog came upon us and stepped right on the shiny propeller blades. A cheerful pet owner caught up to him, and we had a brief chat about dogs and mud. Nothing was said about our expensive flying camera. After they departed we held our breath as the stealthy drone hovered 525 feet above Wave Hill to capture its beauty.

We did that for the book you hold in your hands. Photographer Joe Conzo and I wanted to create a book for you about the Bronx that had never been created before. The Bronx isn't like the other four boroughs of New York City – or really any other place in the world – and we set out to put that claim to the test. I took the title of this series to heart when picking the 111 places to include. It says "Must Not Miss." We knocked on doors, climbed over fences, and walked many blocks to reach the "must" destinations.

Here are 111 off-the-radar places that celebrate the Bronx that we want you to explore: from where George Washington ate lunch to the rec center Jennifer Lopez danced, where to eat the best mechado and find exclusive Jordans, to seek out beer breweries, romantic parks, and graffiti murals. If you want American history, this is where patriots fought and died in Van Cortlandt Park. Hip-hop was born here. The borough motto, from Virgil, *No cede malis* ("Do not yield to evil") didn't register with everyone, including the likes of Bronx bootlegger Dutch Schultz and kidnapper Bruno Richard Hauptmann who hailed from the borough.

Taking the 6 train to Pelham Bay Park, I look down at the tidy homes, pulsating lights of corner stores, chicken shops, and school after school. I am here to document a place you must visit. I am writing a book the Bronx will be proud of. Let it guide you.

Welcome to Da Bronx.

*Kevin C. Fitzpatrick*

# 111 Places

# 1__ 1st Andrew Carnegie Library

*Billionaire's donation supports a community*

New York City will eternally be grateful to steel magnate Andrew Carnegie because his fortune built the majority of the public libraries in use today. In 1901, the philanthropist donated millions of dollars to build 65 branch libraries. He pointed to a map of the city and said a free library should be established so that nobody had to walk more than a quarter of a mile to get good books free of charge. In 1905, Mott Haven was the first to see his wish come true. It is not the oldest library in the Bronx – that honor goes to the 1891 Huntington Free Library and Reading Room in Westchester – but Mott Haven has the first branch library in the borough that is part of the New York Public Library system.

This was the first of nine libraries built in the Bronx; eight are still open. The creation of Babb, Cook & Willard, the architects who designed Carnegie's mansion facing Central Park, the three-floor Mott Haven library covers 15,342 square feet and cost $97,000 (about $2.8 million today). The exterior of brick and limestone is in the Classical Revival style. Inside, you can still feel its Gilded Age influences. The ground floor offers a view of the stunning double staircase that leads to the top floors. It's made of black wrought iron (possibly from the local Mott Iron Works) with carved oak banisters. Two vintage, round, cast-iron radiators have been warming up the main reading room for decades.

After World War II, it was a hub for vehicles to distribute books in the area. It was a center for bilingual language outreach by the 1960s. Today, it's a pillar of the neighborhood, offering literacy programs and technology assistance.

The brick and limestone structure was declared an official New York City landmark in 1969. The legacy of Mr. Carnegie's vision lives on with every person who enters this library.

**Address** 321 East 140th Street, Bronx, NY 10454, +1 (718)665-4878, www.nypl.org/
locations/mott-haven | **Getting there** Subway to Third Avenue–138th Street (6 train),
walk four blocks north on Third Avenue | **Hours** Mon–Fri 10am–7pm, Sat 10am–5pm |
**Tip** The Bronx Arts Space on the same block has an artists' gallery and also offers writers'
workshops (305 West 140th Street, Bronx, NY 10454, www.bronxartspace.com).

# 2___239 Play

*Every day is a toy story*

City Island residents Dan Treiber and Reina Mia Brill took a love of vintage toys and 1980s nostalgia and turned it into a thriving business inside a 1900s commercial building. The couple began their operation at the popular Brooklyn Flea as Dan's Parents' House and moved into the bricks-and-mortar shop in 2016.

Inside the store on the corner of City Island Avenue and Schofield Street is a world of pop culture and kitsch that draws devotees to the quirky shop. With an old wood floor and tin ceiling, the sprawling shop is overflowing with metal and plastic reminders of your childhood.

You will find antique bottles, glasses, G.I. Joes, Hess trucks, LP records, patches, signs, Star Wars galore, and wrestling action figures. "It's always a walk back in time," says Nick Mariotis, manning the store. "Not only are you in a 150-year-old building, you're seeing the stuff from when you were a kid. We're glad we can bring that back to City Islanders and others."

"I'm looking for Wonder Woman," a customer asked Nick. It was clear she was looking for Lynda Carter era, not Gal Gadot. Shelves of plastic superheroes and sci-fi creatures were searched. Unfortunately the shop was temporarily bare in the Amazon department. "The best we have is this Super Friends," Nick helpfully offered. "You could cut the rest out."

The shop is also a gathering spot. 239 Play has special events during the year that are always a hit in the neighborhood. In May is the pizza and beer anniversary party, and the annual Christmas season is jolly good because the store is selling the toys Santa forgot to deliver in 1977. If old toys and games are not your cup of tea, Dan sells a series of folk art pieces made from recycled scrap metal. Vintage metal letters spell *CITY ISLAND*. License plates snipped to be keychains are among some of the treasures tucked in the back.

**Address** 239 City Island Avenue, Bronx, NY 10464, +1 (917)596-0320, www.dansparentshouse.com | **Getting there** Subway to Pelham Bay Park (6 train), transfer to bus Bx29 to City Island Avenue/Schofield Street | **Hours** Sat, Sun, Mon, Wed & Thu 11am–7pm, Fri by appointment only | **Tip** While on the island, you enjoy performances by local actors in community theater. Since 1999, the City Island Theatre Group has produced plays in the landmark Grace Episcopal Church Hall, built in 1862 (116 City Island Avenue, Bronx, NY 10464, www.cityislandtheatergroup.com).

# 3_5 Organized Crime Families
*Where the mob rose to power*

Anyone who has watched *The Godfather* movies knows that organized crime in the 20th century was truly a "family" business. The real-life mafia (or Cosa Nostra) created the Five Families of New York City in the Bronx during the Depression. The roots of the mobsters are all tied to a sit-down meeting in Belmont that created what we call the Mob today.

In 1931, a gathering was held in a rented hall near Washington Avenue and about East 187th Street. The building is no longer there, but if it still existed, it would be the number one crime landmark in any history book. Sicilian crime boss Salvatore Maranzano called the meeting and appointed himself *capo di tutti capi*, "boss of all bosses." He chose his four handpicked lieutenants to divide up local crime operations: Joseph Bonanno, Tommaso "Tommy" Gagliano, Charles "Lucky" Luciano, and Vincent Mangano. That meeting put an end to a bloody war for control of bootlegging, gambling, and other rackets. The crime families are still in existence, nearly ninety years later. Maranzano established a system following the model used in Italy. Each family would organize under one boss. Under the boss would be an underboss, lieutenants (*caporegime*), and soldiers; these would be "made" men loyal to their boss. Maranzano was murdered soon after the meeting at the hands of Lucky Luciano. All of this drama was used by author Mario Puzo as the basis for *The Godfather*.

The rise of organized crime came at the same time as the rise in power of J. Edgar Hoover and the FBI. The director denied that organized crime existed, and his bureau focused primarily on catching kidnappers and bank robbers. All of this changed when Luciano launched "The Commission," and Meyer Lansky and Bugsy Siegel formed Murder Incorporated. Ever since then, the FBI has battled organized crime. This street corner is the birthplace of that conflict.

Address Intersection of Washington Avenue and East 187th Street, Bronx, NY 10458 |
Getting there Subway to Fordham Road (B, D train), Metro-North Railroad to Fordham |
Hours Unrestricted | Tip You can recreate your own sit-down meeting by venturing to Zero
Otto Nove. It serves Southern Italian dishes in a large and airy space (2357 Arthur Avenue,
Bronx, NY 10458, www.zeroottonove.com/locations/bronx).

# 4__6BASE

*Studios and exhibitions support the arts*

A rotating artist studio and exhibition space in the South Bronx, 6BASE was launched by Marina Gluckman in June 2016. This 1931 industrial warehouse was converted into the studios, and 6BASE occupies a floor of the warehouse in a loft that is divided into seven bays. 6BASE is in one of these bays, about 450 square feet, and the others are the artists' studios. Artists are given a month of free access, and then they are invited to present what they created to the public at an open exhibition.

The studio provides artists, from around the world and locals alike, an opportunity to create and exhibit their work in a small gallery setting. The studio and exhibition program works to bring a positive environment for creators, be they artists, musicians, or writers. They have a space not only to create, but to invite the public to come see what has been made here on East 136th Street. The mission of 6BASE is to build a network of artists to engage with each other and other people in the Bronx.

Gluckman has a master's degree in art history from Hunter College, a background in the gallery world, and was a guest curator for The Other Art Fair in Brooklyn. Three years ago, she positioned the studio in a neighborhood seeing more artists come into the South Bronx. 6BASE is located in a steadily rising area of studios and galleries (see ch. 105). The movement is bringing the Chelsea art scene to Port Morris. The exhibitions and opening-night events are big draws to the neighborhood, attracting personalities and fans from the creative world.

The art exhibited here has included all styles and mediums. Among those who have been in the program are painter Chelsea Cater, sculptor Jody Joyner, and painter Bruno Smith. 6BASE recently curated a group show of 14 Bronx artists. Among them were Bernard Beckford, Michele Brody, Chen Carrasco, and Estelle Maisonett.

Address 728 East 136th Street, Suite 6B, Bronx, NY 10454, www.6base.nyc, info@6base.nyc | Getting there Subway to Cypress Avenue (6 train) | Hours Sat & Sun noon – 6pm or by appointment | Tip Around the corner, you can see wall art by mural kings TATS Cru. Their work serves as a gateway to the South Bronx and is a perfect selfie spot (bridge across from 1 Bruckner Boulevard, Bronx, NY 10454, www.tatscru.net).

# 5 Abandoned Railway Line

*This train in the woods will never arrive*

In 1870, a railroad line was created to serve what is Van Cortlandt Park today. It was abandoned in 1958 due to a drop in ridership. Now hikers can explore the platform, track bed, steel bridges, and railroad remnants still standing in the middle of the park.

After the Civil War, the population of New York City exploded as immigrants poured into the United States. Railroads pushed commuter lines east of the Harlem River along the Putnam Line to run north. The railway was later merged with the mightiest railroad of the era, the New York Central, which was easily identified by its distinctive oval logo and beautifully decorated coaches. As family estates in the Bronx were broken up and sold to developers, neighborhoods sprang up, fed by the steam trains that could bring commuters quickly to Manhattan. As Westchester and Putnam Counties to the north grew, so did the demand for commuter lines.

The small branch line that served the Bronx and Westchester County had only a dozen modest stations and terminated in Yonkers at Getty Square. Riders of the "Put" would board at Grand Central Terminal and change trains in High Bridge until passenger service ceased in 1958. Crews ripped out the steel tracks but left the rest of the railroad infrastructure in place.

Ayinde Stevens, a tour guide and railroad buff, thinks it's too bad the Put was removed. "It would probably make parts of the Bronx more accessible now," he says. "I'm actually surprised it didn't get converted to the subway."

Today, it is easy to locate the trail that leads you to the abandoned railway line. In Van Cortlandt Park, walk east from the 1 Train at the East 242nd Street station. Look for signs for the Old Putnam Trail east of the Van Cortlandt Nature Center. Along the trail, you'll find the abandoned platform and bridges as you follow the same route that many commuters took beginning 150 years ago.

**Address** Old Putnam Trail, Bronx, NY 10471, www.nycgovparks.org/parks/vancortlandtpark |
**Getting there** Subway to East 242nd Street (1 train) | **Hours** Daily 6am–10pm | **Tip**
Learn more about the area flora and wildlife at the Van Cortlandt Nature Center next to
the trail. Park rangers lead guided tours, and it's a hotspot for birdwatchers to gather (Van
Cortlandt Nature Center, Bronx, NY 10471, www.nycgo.com/venues/van-cortlandt-nature-
center-riverdale).

# 6 Abe Lincoln Sculpted Here

*From Mott Haven came the grandest memorial*

The most famous memorial in Washington, D.C., which annually gets eight million visitors, has a humble creation story. The Lincoln Memorial was carved by a team of brothers in Mott Haven. In the first decades of the 20th century, their Piccirilli Brothers were the most sought-after stone carvers in America. They created memorials and monuments all over New York, but their most famous work was carved in the Bronx in 1919.

In 1888, master carver Giuseppe Piccirilli emigrated from Massa Carrara, Italy, with his wife Barbara and their six sons and daughter. Sons Attilio and Furio were the most famous and carved the USS *Maine* memorial in Columbus Circle and the two lions in front of the New York Public Library. The other four brothers, Ferruccio, Getullio, Masaniello, Orazio (and maybe their sister, Jole), worked with 100 other Italian carvers in the studio on 142nd Street between Willis and Brook Avenues. The Piccirilli Brothers created so many famous sculptures – the list is as long as your arm.

But the Lincoln Memorial project is their most impressive. The white Georgia marble was sent to the Bronx via boat. The 28 blocks were transformed into intricate pieces following the design of sculptor Daniel Chester French. The blocks were hoisted into place and fit perfectly – the seams are nearly invisible. Originally, the memorial was only planned to be 10' tall, but it ended up being 19' tall from head to foot. Installation was completed in 1920, and the memorial was dedicated two years later. It quickly became a powerful symbol for the nation.

The brothers might have slipped into the cracks of history if not for the work of local history buffs. In the last few years a plaque and street-naming honor the family. The one place the name Piccirilli is not carved is on their most famous work. The Lincoln Memorial Commission said the surname was "too Italian" to include on the base.

Address Piccirilli Place on the corner of 142nd Street and Willis Avenue, Bronx, NY 10454 | Getting there Subway to Brook Avenue (6 train) | Hours Unrestricted | Tip The Piccirilli Brothers never left the Bronx. Most of the family is interred in the Rose Hill Plot in Woodlawn Cemetery. Of course, their headstones are beautifully carved, but don't miss the sculpture on their mama's grave of a mother comforting a small child (4199 Webster Avenue, Bronx, NY 10470, www.thewoodlawncemetery.org).

# 7 — Alexander Antiques

*Looking for a love seat to love you back*

If you believe, as journalist Natalie Morales does, that "furniture is meant to be used and enjoyed," then picking out a new couch or chest of drawers makes for one fun excursion. The hunt for the right piece for your home is just as much of a good time as slapping your credit card on the counter and taking it home. Antique and vintage buyers all know this feeling.

In the 1980s, shoppers scoured the South Bronx Antique Row in Mott Haven, which was a must-visit for anyone looking for treasures. Multiple stores on Bruckner Boulevard have since shuttered, and the lone remaining store is Alexander Antiques. Off the Major Deegan Expressway, the area was historically called the Piano District. But don't look for old pianos at Alexander Antiques. Instead, you'll find furniture from when *I Love Lucy* was the top show on TV. Daily, it sees delivery men unloading bed frames, bureaus, dressers, and more to the sidewalk. The former contents of area homes are stacked from floor to ceiling inside the store. This is the place to look for glass doorknobs, mid-century furniture, wall sconces, rugs, and picture frames.

Insiders say the entrepreneurial spirit of the neighborhood is what started the short-lived Antiques Row. Spying the Connecticut license plates of cars heading north on the Deegan, it dawned on the purveyors of antiques that perhaps these passing motorists might stop for a little treasure hunting. Word spread, and Antiques Row took root. Savvy antique shoppers know to hit the stores at the end of the month when people move out of apartments and cast off old furniture.

When Beatstro (see ch. 12) opened in 2018 around the corner, the partners wanted to give it the vibe of a 1970s apartment. They shopped here at Alexander Antiques to get the right kind of chairs and furniture for the lounge. You'll find all types of treasures there. Call ahead to make sure the store is open.

Address 41 Bruckner Boulevard, Bronx, NY 10454, +1 (718)401-8629 | Getting there Subway to Third Avenue–138th Street (6 train) | Hours By appointment only | Tip Major William F. Deegan not only has eight miles of a highway named for him, he also has a rock. A seven-and-a-half-foot-tall Concord granite boulder was dedicated in 1935 to the army engineer and architect from New York. It's in Deegan Park, a former railroad yard (Junction of East 138th Street, the Expressway, and the Grand Concourse, www.nycgovparks.org/parks/deegan-rock).

# 8 Andrew Freedman Home

*Goodwill gesture a century ago leads to art today*

This is the story of a multimillionaire who was so grateful he didn't lose every bit of his fortune in Wall Street disasters that he created a retirement home for people like himself.

Andrew Freedman was born poor in Manhattan in 1860 and rose to great wealth by investing in real estate and railroads. In 1920, he was the first director of the Interborough Rapid Transit Company (IRT) launched by his friend August Belmont, Jr. *The New York Times* wrote that Freedman "did more perhaps than any other man to make possible the subway system in this city." He was a power-broker in Tammany Hall and a confidant of city mayors and ward bosses. Freedman owned the New York Giants baseball club when they were the biggest draw in the game.

Freedman never married, and died of a stroke in 1915. Despite owning mansions in two states, he died in his bachelor apartment above his favorite Times Square restaurant. Perhaps that factored into his will, as his legacy would be to take care of others at the Andrew Freedman Home for the elderly, which operated for 80 years before closing its doors. After the last resident was relocated in the 1980s, the building was renovated as a cultural center and event space.

Andrew Freedman Home (AFH) is now a destination for an eclectic mix of arts programming. It launched an artist residency program in 2016, providing free private studio space in exchange for the artists working a few hours a week leading projects and workshops. The program has attracted designers, musicians, and painters. AFH offers free classes for young people in art, cooking, dance, music, photography, and poetry. The playhouse presents locally written and produced dance, drama, and performances. AFH holds public events throughout year, from DJ nights, music, and arts festivals to poetry readings. A century after his death, Freedman's legacy inspires creativity on the Grand Concourse.

Address 1125 Grand Concourse, Bronx, NY 10452, +1 (718)410-6735,
www.andrewfreedmanhome.org, afharts@gmail.com | Getting there Subway to 167th
Street (B, D train), bus Bx1, Bx2 to Grand Concourse/McClellan Street | Hours Mon–Thu
9am–7pm, Fri 9am–5pm, Sat 10am–5:30pm | Tip Get in touch with feathered friends at
the Dred Scott Bird Sanctuary a few blocks north. Troy and Patricia Lancaster founded it
when their family cleared an ugly lot and planted greenery to attract birds. Today, NYC
manages the site that's become a neighborhood jewel (Grant Avenue and East 169th Street,
Bronx, NY 10456, www.dsbs1.org).

# 9  Artuso Pastry Shop
*Cookies from heaven*

Italians began moving into Belmont in large numbers in the early 1910s as immigrants left Lower Manhattan for a new beginning in the Bronx. Some went to work building the subway system as it expanded north. Today, that Italian influence is most conspicuous on the food culture in this neighborhood. One pastry shop of note is a longtime favorite and has a 70-year history of baking cookies and wedding cakes.

Launched by Vincent Artuso after he returned from serving in World War II, Artuso Pastry Shop is still in the family and has expanded into multiple stores and covers half a city block. Each day, a delectable array of cookies comes from the oven in all shapes and sizes. On display are cases with row upon row of cookies and pastries for sale by the pound or piece. Among the mouth-watering fare are colorfully decorated almond cookies, butter cookies, chocolate chip swirls, éclairs, half-dipped chocolate hearts, long cat's tongues, rum baba, and sprinkles of every color in the rainbow. The most divine – and tempting – is a wedge of chocolate mousse with a cookie buried halfway on top.

The shop has a few tables where visitors can tuck into their pastries on the premises. Enjoy a coffee or espresso – the espresso con panna comes with a dab of fresh whipped cream.

Artuso's has had its share of ups and downs over the years, but the lines to get in the door are always long. The shop saw a bonanza when it debuted "Pope Cookies" for Pope Francis and Pope Benedict XVI; customers came from out of state to get their hands on the Holy Father. The business recovered from hardships, including a devastating fire in 1957 and a calamitous blaze that destroyed their retail bakery in Mount Vernon in 2014. The business is stronger than ever and now sells its products to supermarkets and wholesale customers. Like cake? Take a peek at their albums of past cake creations.

Address 670 East 187th Street, Bronx, NY 10458, +1 (718)367-2515, www.artusopastry.com |
Getting there Subway to Pelham Parkway (2, 5 train), and transfer to bus Bx12 to East
Fordham Road / Hoffman Street and walk south on Arthur Avenue; or subway to Fordham
Road (B, D train), and transfer to Bx22 to East Fordham Road / Cambrelant Avenue |
Hours Mon – Fri 7am – 8:30pm, Sat 7am – 9pm, Sun 7am – 6:30pm | Tip There are more
than 25 merchants in the Arthur Avenue neighborhood that keep alive the Italian traditions.
Every September is the annual Ferragosto, a celebration of Italian culture and food
(www.arthuravenuebronx.com).

# 10___Bartow-Pell Mansion
*Find the house hidden in the woods*

It's a trip to the 19th century when you walk through the door of this beautiful country house situated in the heart of Pelham Bay Park. The period interiors are original, and the house museum has an outstanding collection of art and furniture. The home is open for intimate music performances, guided tours, and special events. The gardens and landscaping are stunning and are frequently used for fashion shoots.

Robert and Marie Lorillard Bartow moved into the Revolutionary War-era country house in the 1830s and they set about renovating it. A successful book publisher, Robert was a descendant of Thomas Pell, an English colonist who in 1654 claimed most of the Bronx and southern Westchester County. Members of the Pell family are buried on the grounds.

Pelham Bay Park was established in 1888, and New York City bought up all of the old mansions and homes in the park boundaries. In 1914, the International Garden Club rescued the Bartow-Pell Mansion and returned it to its former glory. Renting it from the city, the club hired Delano and Aldrich, who had worked for the Rockefellers, to give it a facelift. The club installed period rooms and later borrowed pieces from museums to set the mood, and they planted the gardens to bring the house to a new level of graciousness and beauty.

We are lucky this mansion survives to this day, as in the 1930s, Parks Commissioner Robert Moses ordered other fine homes in the surrounding forest to be razed.

Today, the Bartow-Pell Mansion is one of the most spectacular house museums on the East Coast. It has a carefully preserved interior that is open to tour and visit. The gardens attract visitors to the wide collection of flowers and fauna, and the design is spectacular. Don't miss the carriage house. Take time to walk the surrounding property and look for the Pell family burial grounds, as they are the ones who started it all.

Address 895 Shore Road, Bronx, NY 10464, +1 (718)885-1461,
www.bartowpellmansionmuseum.org | **Getting there** Subway to Pelham Bay Park (6 train),
then bus Bx29 to City Island Road/Shore Road | **Hours** House and Carriage House
Wed, Sat & Sun noon–4pm; Grounds daily 8:30am–dusk | **Tip** Forty acres of Pelham
Bay Park are named Huntington Woods after the property's former owner, millionaire
philanthropist Archer Huntington. His mansion was demolished, and all that's left is the
family's animal cemetery for dogs, horses, and other pets. To locate it, follow the path at
Library and Watt Avenues near the NYPD stables (www.nycgovparks.org/parks/pelham-
bay-park/monuments/757).

# 11  Battle of Westchester Creek

*Rebel forces fought on Bronx territory*

In the parking lot of White Castle is an historic marker, not for a famous hamburger, but for General George Washington. He didn't eat here. Rather, on October 12, 1776, this was the site of a battle between the British Army and Delaware riflemen. This was crucial to the rebellion, and the advancing British did not trap Washington's forces.

At this time, Westchester Square was a village in Westchester County. A creek with a tidal mill was vital to the village. In early October 1776, Washington learned of British commander-in-chief General William Howe's plan to land his forces on the North Shore of Long Island Sound to cut off the Americans at the rear. Washington chose General William Heath to halt the advance in Westchester. Heath inspected the area and chose to defend the mill and causeway. He picked 25 men and stationed them here with orders to destroy a footbridge if the British advanced. General Washington and his forces moved west to camp in White Plains. The rebels waited for the attack.

The British landed 80 to 90 boatloads of men at Throggs Point, a finger of land extending into the Long Island Sound. The British came through what is today west of Hutchinson River Parkway and Bruckner Boulevard and marched on to Westchester. By the time they reached the creek, the rebels had wrecked the small bridge. They opened fire on the British from the mill and causeway. General Howe was furious and was forced to retreat. He would go on to attack Pelham a few days later. However, the Americans gained momentum in the fight, Washington was able to move his forces, and the rebellion wasn't stopped at this early stage in the war.

Nearly 250 years later, all of the bucolic greenery and creek is gone, replaced by modern city life. A granite marker is placed close to the location of the action.

Address 2900 East Tremont Avenue, Bronx, NY 10461 | Getting there  Subway to West-chester Square – East Tremont Avenue (6 train) | Hours Unrestricted | Tip Add some history to your home with bric-a-brac, furniture, lamps, signs, and glassware that you didn't know you needed at Vintage In The Square (2587 Saint Raymond Avenue, Bronx, NY 10461).

# 12  Beatstro

*Putting the beats into brunch*

There are many places to get French toast around the world, but there is one spot that serves it soaked in rum with a side of fresh beats. The brainchild of Alfredo Angueira and Julio Martinez, Beatstro is a bar/restaurant they dropped on Mott Haven in 2018. Its doors are open to everyone, no matter where you're from, whether its public housing or a sleek condo. Beatstro offers comfort food, a dance floor, and DJs.

You think you're walking into a used record shop with bins of old-school LPs. But pass through a curtain, and you're in the main room with chandeliers, graffiti murals, and throwback photos to the birth of hip hop. A long subway mural by TMT Crew is one of many original pieces. The comfy furniture came via Alexander Antiques (see ch. 7) around the corner.

"Beatstro is the kind of place where you talk about your childhood and what street you grew up on. What your favorite songs were, DJs, and shows that meant a lot to you," says chef Leonardo Marino. "The food is authentic and reflects the area. What we serve has notes of soul food on a journey from the South to here. Our partners are Dominican, Puerto Rican, Italian, and Southern. We serve all the things we like to eat. Ricky has chicken in his background, so we got a pressure fryer for fried chicken. Anyone that takes their chicken seriously has one."

What is driving visitors across streets and bridges to Beatstro are the weekend brunches that start at 11am and may wrap up at 5pm. "Try the steak and eggs mangu with mashed plantains just like in the DR," says bartender Celina Santana. "You don't have many places like this in the Bronx. The crowd we're attracting is what's special – a chill laid-back vibe. You can actually sit at the bar, talk and enjoy the atmosphere." Try a Method Manhattan, a version of the classic cocktail made with rye, Benedictine, and orange.

Address 135 Alexander Avenue, Bronx, NY 10454, +1 (718)489-9397, www.beatstro.com, contact@beatstro.com | Getting there Subway to Third Avenue – 138th Street (6 train), bus Bx33 to East 138th Street / Alexander Avenue | Hours Mon – Thu 4pm – 2am, Fri 4pm – 3am, Sat 11:30 – 3am, Sun 11:30am – midnight | Tip Shop local in the boutique 9J for Bronx-handmade embroidered jackets and shirts, artwork, and handmade jewelry that line the walls and displays (41 Bruckner Boulevard, Bronx, NY 10454, www.9jstudio.com).

# 13 Betty Boop's School

*Clason Point native Helen Kane became a cartoon*

Where would the world be without Betty Boop in it? The cartoony vixen-next-door – pixie bob, apple cheeks, big eyes – is based on a Catholic schoolgirl from the Bronx who attended Saint Anselm's. The real-life inspiration for Betty is a petite singer from a working-class family in Clason Point. Born Helen Clare Schroeder on August 4, 1904, she got her start at Saint Anselm's. Her mom, Ellen, scraped together $3 for a costume so her daughter could properly portray a queen in a school play.

At 17, she went to London with the Marx Brothers. As Helen Kane, she became a star in the waning days of vaudeville. While rehearsing the song "That's My Weakness Now" at the Paramount Theatre in Times Square, she closed it in a squeaky baby voice, "boop-boop-a-doop." The cute but "meaningless" line became her catchphrase. Helen became a recording star, appeared in nine films, and was a national celebrity in the Jazz Age.

Max Fleischer Studios' animators appropriated her likeness and voice in 1930. The first Betty Boop appearance was the short film *Dizzy Dishes*. A series of hit cartoons followed, and Betty Boop eclipsed Helen Kane. In 1932, Helen sued the studio for $250,000 (about $4.5 million today), claiming her likeness rights were appropriated. "She has played the role or part of a very young but seductive female who uses in her speech and songs an exaggerated lisp and a childish voice and manner," her lawsuit declares, "coupled with a mature physique, are well calculated to portray a feminine type popularly known as the 'baby vamp'." Helen was out-lawyered, and she lost the case.

Helen married four times and squandered a fortune. She retired to Queens but visited the Bronx often. "There's no more boyish form now, you know," she said. "Plump girls are coming back." After a long battle with breast cancer, Helen died penniless in Jackson Heights on September 27, 1966. She was 61.

Address 685 Tinton Avenue, Bronx, NY 10455, www.stanselmbx.org | Getting there Subway to Jackson Avenue (2, 5 train) | Tip Go play in Bill Rainey Park, which borders Dawson Street, where Helen grew up. Her house and other tenements nearby were demolished to build this eight-acre park in 1986 (bordered by Dawson and Beck Streets, Interval and Longwood Avenues, Bronx, NY 10459, www.nycgovparks.org/parks/rainey-park).

# 14__Big Pun Mural

*Changing wall art to Longwood rapper*

The street art tribute to rapper Big Pun is a nearly annual affair in aerosol. Almost every year, in time for his November 10 birthday, a new mural replaces one that went up the previous year. TATS Cru, the international graffiti all-stars (see ch. 105) were the first of many to have painted the mural on Rogers Place in Longwood. For more than 10 years, a rotating cast of guest street artists has taken turns with TATS to add their tributes.

Christopher Lee Carlos Rios (1971–2000) got his stage name Big Pun (short for Big Punisher) when he launched his rapping career. He had a Dickensian childhood, with his teenage years spent struggling to survive in the South Bronx. Big Pun turned a bleak early life marred by multiple setbacks into a music career that spoke to his experience coming from poverty. He was a gifted rapper who got his break when he recorded with another Bronx hardcore rapper, Fat Joe. His skills were multisyllabic schemes and alliteration. He became the first Latino MC to be certified platinum, selling over half a million albums. Among Big Pun's biggest hits were "Still Not A Player" and "100%."

In 1999, he was nominated for a Grammy Award for Best Rap Album. On "Glamour Life," he rapped:

*The glamour life, this life I live is trife as shit*
*Least my wife and kid got somewhere nice to live*
*I used to live in the gutter, me and my mother*
*Now she's fifty years old, pushing a Hummer*

His size, at close to 700 pounds, contributed to his brief career and short life. He was only 28 when he died of heart disease. Sadly, Big Pun is now more famous in death than he was in life.

The wall of Cache jewelry store is the spot where Big Pun was famously photographed. The first memorial included the work of artists BG183, BIO, How, Nicer, and Nosm. Today, it's one of the biggest tour bus attractions in the borough.

Address 910 Rogers Place, Bronx, NY 10459 | Getting there Subway to Interval Avenue (2, 5 train) | Hours Unrestricted | Tip The nearby shopping district on Southern Boulevard is a destination for affordable clothing, electronics, shoes, and discount stores. There are at least 10 jewelry shops. The boulevard is filled with Caribbean restaurants, so shop hungry (Southern Boulevard, Bronx, NY 10459, www.southernblvdbid.com).

# 15 The Bronx Brewery

*Bringing back a beloved lost industry*

If asked to name a beverage associated with the Bronx, would anyone think of beer? There is a famous gin cocktail named for the borough – the bartender who created it said the residents of the Bronx Zoo reminded him of his customers. However, brewing beer in the borough has roots going back to the colonial era. German immigrants developed and grew the industry in the 19th century, and long-lost breweries such as Ebling's, Eichler's, and Hupfel's brewed beer for almost 100 years. The bubbles ceased to flow during Prohibition, killing the industry. In 2011, the Bronx Brewery revived the tradition in the South Bronx with a modern brewery and a cozy taproom.

Among the craft beer offerings they brew year-round are an American pale ale, No Resolutions India pale ale, Slow Your Roll Session India pale ale, and Kolsch Golden Ale. There are seasonals and collaborations with other brewers, along with what they call "up and comers" to taste new products. The Steep Aside pale ale was made with tea and chamomile. The cans and packaging are also Bronx-centric, with borough artists and graphic designers creating the colorful branding and artwork. The first tapped with painter-sculptor Natalie Collette Wood, ostensibly creating a small, rotating art gallery on a can.

Visitors can watch the beer being brewed in giant vats and then repair to the attached taproom for some sampling. The taproom has a dozen beers on tap and 40 seats for customers. Its industrial design and benches are in keeping with the brewery's handmade vibe. The brewery's backyard is open April–October, six days a week, and the brewery hosts outdoor ticketed parties with local food vendors and DJs. When the weather gets cold, there are open mic nights indoors. Free public tours are offered on weekends; check website for schedule. You can also book a private tour and tasting for small groups.

Address 856 East 136th Street, Bronx, NY 10454, +1 (718)402-1000,
www.thcbronxbrewery.com, brewers@thebronxbrewery.com | Getting there Subway
to Cypress Avenue (6 train) | Hours Check website for schedule | Tip The Bronx
County Historical Society and Woodlawn Cemetery partner to offer trolley tours of
beer history. Tours begin in the cemetery where many brewers are interred, travel to the
locations of former breweries, and then take everyone to the new breweries and taprooms
(www.bronxhistoricalsociety.org).

# 16__Bronx Documentary Center

*Creating the next generation of photographers*

The Bronx Documentary Center (BDC) was born out of tragedy and heartbreaking loss. Founded by Executive Director Mike Kamber, the center is a vibrant oasis of creativity and a living institution that keeps alive the ideals of a conflict photographer who died before the center opened, Tim Hetherington. Hetherington was an award-winning photographer who spent a quarter century in war zones around the world. He and Mike discussed the BDC idea while on assignment.

"I was working with Tim overseas in Africa and the Middle East," Mike says. "We were looking at programs to train young photographers in Africa, and we thought, if we can do it here, why not in the Bronx? Tim was killed in 2011. He had the ideas and programs. We are doing exactly what we talked about."

Mike returned to the US, and with the savings he'd earned working in places like Iraq, he bought the ideal spot: a landmark 1871 building that had been a German meeting hall. It has gallery exhibition space, offices, workrooms, and quarters for hosting visiting photographers. "We opened in June 2011 right after he was killed," Mike recalled. "His bloodstains were on (his work) from Libya. For our first exhibition, we showed projections of his works."

"When we began, we found refurbished Canon cameras for 50 bucks," Mike continued. "We wanted to take kids off the street and teach them photography."

BDC holds five to seven public exhibitions a year, a mix of Bronx shows with national and international exhibitions. "We want (kids and visitors) to learn about the Bronx, and learn about the world. People have been coming in for seven years. We're now part of the neighborhood," Mike says.

**Address** 614 Courtlandt Avenue, Bronx, NY 10451, +1 (718)993-3512, www.bronxdoc.org |
**Getting there** Subway to Third Avenue–149th Street (2, 5 train). Walk up 149th Street
one block and make a right on Courtlandt Avenue. Walk two blocks to the mansion on the
corner of 151st Street. | **Hours** Thu & Fri 3–7pm, Sat & Sun 1–5pm, check website for
extended hours and exceptions | **Tip** See how much authentic Mexican food you can devour
at Xochimilco Family Restaurant. Try a cemita (sesame seed roll sandwich) or small rounded
handmade tortillas called sopes (653 Melrose Avenue, Bronx, NY 10455, www.xochimilco-
family-restaurant.business.site).

# 17__Bronx Native

*Wear your heart on your sleeve*

You know that T-shirt that says I ♥ NY? Well, Bronx Native has come up with a way to beat that. It's a shirt that plainly states "El Bronx" and joins one of many items selling like mad from the tiny shop in Mott Haven. Behind the store and brand are the brother and sister team Amaurys and Roselyn Grullon. Bronx Native is much more than a clothing brand. Amaurys and Roselyn have created and cultivated a meeting spot for the community. Alexandria Ocasio-Cortez launched her successful run for Congress at the shop. You can see the tag she left on the wall in silver marker, *OCASIO2018*.

Amaurys explained, "We love our people and our home. We got tired of hearing all this negativity coming from others who don't really know what the Bronx is really about," says Amaurys. "It started as a conversation my sister and I had. We really wanted to find merchandise that represented the Bronx – something that utilized the culture, history, and also was visually appealing. We couldn't find anything. I said, this is kind of weird. This is the Mecca, the birthplace of culture. We created great things and still we're put to the side. So we thought, since we have the skills in design and media, and the ideas, let's just do this. My sister is a fashion design student at Parsons. We wanted to become a brand that did more than just Bronx-based merchandise."

Bronx Native quickly became a gathering spot after launching in 2017. "We call it a cultural hub," Amaurys said. "This is a place where anyone who comes in can tag up the walls. We host live music events, community events. We want to do whatever we can for the Bronx."

The store stocks Bronx-centric caps, shirts, and sweatshirts. Because the space in the shop is limited, events spill out into the sidewalk. Performers, poets, rappers, singers, and musicians drop by. "They gather to connect and network, it's something beautiful," Amaurys says.

Address 127 Lincoln Avenue, Bronx, NY 10454, +1 (646)598-4505, www.bronxnative.com, info@bronxnative.com | **Getting there** Subway to Third Avenue–138th Street (6 train), walk south on Lincoln Avenue five blocks | **Tip** Walk across Bruckner Boulevard to see amazing street art around Lincoln and Alexander Avenues.

# 18 Bronx Public

*Filling up on food and good times*

A group of eight adults are huddled around a table, standing up and laughing. You can't hear what they are saying, but from across the bar it appears they are either gambling or playing blackjack. Upon closer inspection, and after a look over some shoulders, the excitement is actually over a fast-paced game of Uno, matching colors and numbers. What gives? On the next table is a container of Jenga blocks. The Bronx Public is the kind of place where DJs are providing the beat and the bartenders are serving up fresh cocktails. The plates of food coming out of the kitchen make your mouth water.

This newcomer is on a mission to be the clubhouse for Bronx friends. It opened in 2017 in a spot that had been a sleepy Irish bar for decades. The walls are covered in graffiti art and images from vintage 1980s street life – call it nostalgia for the golden age of hip-hop. The Knicks and Nets play on the flat screens in the background, the ceiling has exposed beams with graffiti to look up to. The music is a mix of songs from high school in the 1990s and current favorites. It is very, very easy to spot the staff: they are all wearing matching plaid shirts. Being in the Bronx Public is like being at home with your friends over. It's relaxed, and the only loud voices are coming from people welcoming their friends when they walk in.

The kitchen here is worth the trip for dinner. Brunch on the weekends goes till 4pm (make a reservation). They are going to hit you with homemade butter biscuits and banana chocolate French toast. Add a Bloody Mary or mimosa. The lunch and dinner menu is comfort food with a strong Latino flavor, including beef, chicken, and pork dishes. The chicken and waffles is a half chicken on a giant homemade waffle. Check their social media events for a lineup such as "Paint, Sip, and Brunch" adult painting class, live bands, and hip-hop trivia.

Address 170 West 231st Street, Bronx, NY 10463, +1 (718)708-6447, www.thebronxpublic.com | Getting there Subway to 231st Street (1 train), walk one block west | Hours Mon–Fri 3pm–12:30am, Sat & Sun 11:30–3:30am | Tip In 1866, financier and racehorse fan Leonard W. Jerome opened a racecourse nearby. It was wildly successful until it closed in 1894. The racecourse is now the 130-acre Jerome Park Reservoir (West 205th Street and Goulden Avenue, Bronx, NY 10463, www.nycgovparks.org/parks/jerome-park).

# 19 Bronx River Arts Center

*Touching lives by introducing arts to community*

A beautiful gallery space presents emerging artists and professionals working in the Bronx in many different disciplines. It is worth visiting to see what is new in visual arts coming out of the area. For more than 30 years the West Farms community has looked to the Bronx River Arts Center (BRAC) for classes taught by professionals, youth programs, and courses in cartooning, ceramics, drawing, and painting. BRAC houses artists' studios, exhibition spaces, and public programming. BRAC has a mission to bring professional arts programming to a culturally underserved population, and the eye-catching building is home to art classrooms, studios, offices, and gallery spaces. The goal is to use their space as a multi-arts center to fill the community with art and environmental experiences.

The BRAC programs are designed to encourage residents to engage in "creative activism" to help with the revitalization and future of the neighborhood by organizing educational courses for all ages, at low or zero cost. It offers performances of classically inspired, contemporary, experimental, and popular styles to showcase dance, music, performance art, and poetry. Annually in June, BRAC hosts Bronx River Sounds, its performing arts festival. The festival is a popular program to showcase emerging and established groups to bring their performances to a wide audience. For professional artists, BRAC also organizes Bronx Now, a biennial showcase of 16 local artists' paintings, photography, sculpture, and video works.

BRAC is working to launch a creative environment where artists of all types can work side by side. While pursuing their own work, the artists can also engage with the community. On the roof of the building is a landscaped section that absorbs rainwater, acts as a teaching tool, and is an event space as the 2 and 5 trains slide by on the elevated tracks.

**Address** 1087 East Tremont Avenue, Bronx, NY 10460, www.bronxriverart.org |
**Getting there** Subway to West Farms–East Tremont (2, 5 train), walk one block east |
**Hours** Wed–Fri 3–6pm, Sat noon–5pm, only during exhibition dates. Check website
for schedule. | **Tip** Nearby is a tiny park named for community activist Eae James Mitchell,
a cofounder of the Mid-Bronx Desperadoes. In the 1970s when the South Bronx was
devastated, he rescued a dusty vacant lot on 174th Street. The city sold it to him for $1
and he leveled it and cleaned the garbage out himself. When it was ready, he invited the
community to enjoy in (995 East 174th Street, Bronx, NY 10460, www.nycgovparks.org/
parks/mitchell-mall).

# 20__Bug Carousel
*Beetles and bees and crickets – oh my!*

A staple of any fair or amusement park is a carousel, usually featuring stallions and ponies. Carousels have come a long way since they were first manually operated or pulled by ponies in England nearly 200 years ago. The Bronx Zoo, always promoting its core missions of conservation and education, has taken the popular children's ride to a new level.

In 2005 the Bug Carousel made its grand debut, the first permanent carousel in the borough in 65 years. For the opening, the zoo brought in 11 real exterminators, and with raised fly swatters, they launched the carousel with a pledge that not all bugs are bad (the carousel does not have a cockroach).

Handmade by Carousel Works in Mansfield, Ohio, the biggest carousel shop in the world, the Bug Carousel does include 64 different types of insects that riders clamber aboard, including beetles, cicadas, fireflies, grasshoppers, honey bees, ladybugs, and a long-legged praying mantis. Take in the colorful murals that depict the four stages of butterfly and moth metamorphosis: egg, larva, pupa, and adult. This custom-built carousel features two chariots: a *Scarabaeus viettei* (dung beetle) and *Danaus plexippus* (monarch butterfly). Each bug is hand-carved from basswood and painted to match its real-life invertebrate counterpart. To add to the experience, the Wildlife Conservation Society (www.wcs.org) captured wild insect buzzing and humming sounds, which have been added to the festive musical score.

Located between the Dancing Crane Café and Mouse House, the carousel stands ready to lure in new prey at all times when the park is open. It has sliding glass doors to enclose it in cool weather. It's also wheelchair accessible (manual chairs only). Is it popular? More than half a million people ride the Bug Carousel annually. There is a fee to ride, and it is also included in the Total Experience visitor package.

**Address** 2300 Southern Boulevard, Bronx, NY 10460, +1 (718)220-5100, www.bronxzoo.com, guestrelations@wcs.org. | **Getting there** Subway to Pelham Parkway (2, 5 train) and a 10-minute walk to the entrance | **Hours** See website for daily and seasonal hours | **Tip** If nature calls while you're at the zoo, go find the eco-restrooms near the Bronxdale entrance. The zoo installed a Clivus Multrum Composting Toilet System, which composts human waste and saves over a million gallons of water annually with foam flushing (www.clivusmultrum.com/green-building-bronx.php).

# 21 Casa Amadeo Music Shop
*Home of Latin sounds for generations*

Miguel Angel Amadeo – Mike to his fans and friends – is not only the proprietor of Casa Amadeo in Hunts Point. He's a walking encyclopedia of anything connected to Latin music recordings. The roots of the store go back more than 75 years to its predecessor, Casa Hernández, founded by Victoria Hernández. Her brother was bandleader Rafael Hernández Marin, composer of the classic Puerto Rican patriotic song "Lamento Borincano." Mike keeps a shrine to him on the wall.

The shop stocks all styles of Latin music, from bachata to salsa. CDs start with Angel Canales and run to Willie Rosario. Musicians flock here for authentic cowbells, maracas, and drum sticks – *guido* (wood) and *guida* (metal).

Mike started in the music business as a teenager and has composed hundreds of songs. "I wrote my first song at 14, in 1941. I worked for $2 a week in high school in the music business. I've been doing this for 70 years," he explains. In the 1960s, he wrote music and ran another record store and bought this business in 1969. It's his personal connection to the Latin music stars that drives him. He has a song on Celia Cruz' debut record, one of more than 300 he's composed (see ch. 22). "I've written a lot of love songs," he says. "Eighty percent are slow boleros. In the 1960s and 70s when salsa became bigger, I had to take the boleros and double the tempo. It's the same melody but sped up."

Mike is proud of the strong ties his store has to Latin music and still supports the scene today. He doesn't just have a close relationship to the stars who have passed, such as Cruz and Tito Puente, but to newcomers and the hard-working musicians who perform in local clubs. "I figure this is my life," he says.

Ask Mike to bring out one of his scrapbooks. His father played with a young Desi Arnaz. Mike wrote for Julio Jaramillo, the "Frank Sinatra of Ecuador." And go ahead and try out a cowbell.

**Address** 786 Prospect Avenue, Bronx, NY 10455, +1 (718)328-6896 | **Getting there** Subway to Prospect Avenue (2, 5 train), walk across Westchester Avenue | **Hours** Mon–Sat 10:30am–6:30pm | **Tip** A short walk to the street corner of Prospect Avenue and 156th Street is possibly the only mother-daughter double street naming honors in the city. Across from each other are sign tributes to neighborhood activists Dr. Evelina Antonetty and Lorraine Montenegro. These Bronx legends were the driving force behind United Bronx Parents. From school lunches to bilingual education and beyond, the two streets honor women who improved the life of not only the South Bronx, but the city as well (Prospect Avenue and East 156th Street, Bronx, NY 10455).

# 22 __ Celia Cruz Mausoleum

*Salsa over to visit with the Queen*

When Úrsula Hilaria Celia de la Caridad Cruz Alfonso died on July 16, 2003, in New Jersey, it was sad news for her fellow Cubans and music fans. This was Celia Cruz, "Queen of Salsa" and La Guarachera de Cuba, an international recording star beloved by millions. When Cruz's somber mausoleum appeared in 2005 in Woodlawn Cemetery, it quickly became a destination for her fans to visit.

"If you were sitting next to Celia Cruz it was inspirational," says Miguel Angel Amadeo, who composed a song on the first album Cruz made when she immigrated to America, and 50 years later still sells her records at Casa Amadeo (see chapter 21). "Celia was so sweet, everyone loved her. There are other more famous singers, and they sell more, but she was just a wild woman when she got on stage. It was beautiful."

Cruz grew up poor in Havana. She got her start singing with local orchestras and became a radio star fronting a top orchestra, Sonora Matancera. She traveled widely in the 1950s. When Castro came to power, she fled to New York. After Cruz became a US citizen in 1961, Castro barred her from ever returning. Cruz helped propel salsa music to new heights in the 1960s when she toured with Tito Puente. With a larger-than-life stage presence, ever-present smile, and her signature phrase, "Azúcar!" (sugar), her place in Latin music was cemented.

Cruz made more than 75 records, and 23 were certified gold. With hits such as "La Vida Es Un Carnival," she solidified her reputation as a star. In 1994 Cruz became the first Cuban-American to receive a National Medal of Arts by the NEA, presented by President Bill Clinton.

Her grave is in the cemetery's Walnut section. The mausoleum is simple and refined, and Cruz shares it with her husband, Pedro Knight. Peek inside for framed photos. The stained-glass window is "La Caridad del Cobre," Our Lady of Charity, the Patron Saint of Cuba.

Address 4199 Webster Avenue, Bronx, NY 10470, +1 (718)920-0500, www.thewoodlawncemetery.org | Getting there Metro-North to Woodlawn (Harlem Line); subway to Woodlawn (4 train) and walk to Jerome Avenue entrance; or subway to 233rd Street (2, 5 train) and walk three blocks along 233rd Street and cross Webster Avenue to cemetery entrance | Hours Daily 8:30am–4:30pm | Tip There are dozens of musicians buried in Woodlawn Cemetery: Miles Davis, Duke Ellington, Lionel Hampton, W.C. Handy, Max Roach, and Florence Mills, the "Blackbird of Harlem." Get a free map in the cemetery office, or even better, take one of the frequent phonograph tours led by archivist-DJ Michael Cumella (www.michaelcumella.com).

# 23__ Christ Church Riverdale

*More than 150 years of worship and community*

One of the most beautiful churches in the city is hiding in plain sight in Riverdale, where it has served the area since the Civil War era. While the church has some of the finest stained glass and designs of any in the borough, it also has a vibrant congregation of Episcopal/Anglican worshippers. James Onyango, verger and sexton, says, "260 families are members. It's a warm, welcoming, and diverse community. We have many African and Caribbean people. If you join us, you'll feel welcome here."

Christ Church is the work of architect Richard M. Upjohn, son of the better known Richard Upjohn. His 1866 High Victorian Gothic designs for Christ Church include notable fieldstone, local quarried stone, and warm colorful bricks. The beautiful stained-glass windows are outstanding; three windows are original and the others were added later. Inside the chapel, look on the left side for the two windows that are dedicated to Mayor Fiorello La Guardia. A Roman Catholic, he resided in Riverdale and worshipped at Christ Church. The church bell was cast in England and was dedicated upon the safe return of two servicemen in World War II.

When Yankees great Lou Gehrig died in 1941, the baseball team, family, and friends filled the church for his funeral. Babe Ruth honored his friend and teammate by donating an altar rail, which you can see at the front of the church, near the elaborately carved eagle on the pulpit. In 1967, the church was among the first in the borough to be designated by the Landmarks Preservation Committee, which declared, "it is both charming and picturesque and it adds prestige and distinction to the community for which is has served for 100 years."

Christ Church is open on Sunday for two services: 8:30am (hymns omitted), and 11am with music. The congregation is growing with young families and welcomes visitors.

Address 5030 Riverdale Avenue, Bronx, NY 10471, +1 (718)543-1011,
www.christchurchriverdale.org, office@christchurchriverdale.org | Getting there Bus Bx7
to Riverdale Avenue/West 238th Street | Hours Sun 8:30am–noon; check website for
extended hours and exceptions | Tip From the church you can see Bell Tower Park, a
50-foot-tall fieldstone and limestone structure dedicated in 1930 to local World War I
veterans. It's the location for neighborhood Memorial Day ceremonies (West 239th Street
and Riverdale Avenue, Bronx, NY 10471, www.nycgovparks.org/parks/bell-tower-park).

# 24  City Island Nautical Museum

*It's knot what you expect in maritime history*

The modest little museum inside a retired 1898 schoolhouse is one of the finest collections of local life in the Bronx. The City Island Nautical Museum celebrates the nautical heritage of this tiny slice of the borough, with artifacts, boats, books, and memorabilia. Until 1976, it was the local school, and then it was turned into a combination of condos on the upper floors and a museum in the first floor's former classrooms. It's the repository for thousands of pieces of local history, dating back to the Lenape tribe and American Revolution.

Each of the classrooms has a separate theme or exhibition plan. The old seventh grade room holds the Walsh Library, packed with books and periodicals devoted to nautical subjects and maritime history. Look for the models of boats built on City Island: Navy patrol craft, rum runners, and racing sloops. The Nautical Room has a deep collection that speaks to the rich past of yacht building; five America's Cup challengers came from City Island. There are models, photos, sails, tools, and a sailing canoe. The Community Room is packed with items related to life on the island when it was a booming summer resort and waterfront destination. There are hundreds of antiques in the room, from a bishop's chair (he doesn't need it often) to an old icebox. Island life depended on the sea, and this exhibit shows why. Don't miss the schoolroom to see what life was like at the turn of the century.

Highlights not to pass up are the former principal's office, with items from the different island schools, the gallery of folks who played a part in the island's success, a 1937 yacht tender, and a kayak built by German immigrants in the 1930s that shows remarkable craftsmanship. To learn more about City Island history take a guided walking tour organized and led by Barbara Burn Dolensek, the museum's administrator and vice president.

Address 190 Fordham Street, Bronx, NY 10464, +1 (718)885-0008, www.cityislandmuseum.org | Getting there Subway to Pelham Bay Park (6 train), transfer to bus Bx29 to City Island/Fordham Street | Hours Sat & Sun 1–5pm | Tip A short walk away is the waterfront Pelham Cemetery, final resting place of many of the islanders who worked in the oyster and boating business. Some headstones date to the 1860s – look for ones with anchor symbols that mark the graves of seamen (King Avenue and Reville Street, Bronx, NY 10464, www.pelhamcemetery.org).

# 25___Cradle of Hip-Hop

*The blueprints for an entire culture*

It's impossible to go to the street address where the blues started. Or jazz began. Or the first rock 'n' roll show. However, the modest beginnings of hip-hop are right here in the community room of the public housing tower on Sedgwick Avenue. A culture grew up around many cross-pollinating elements (see ch. 77), and this is the spot where the DNA of hip-hop emerged. On August 11, 1973, DJ Kool Herc (Jamaican immigrant Clive Campbell) and his sister Cindy held back-to-school parties for kids in the rec room. Equipped with two turntables and a mixer, Herc introduced the get-down samples to the dance floor.

DJ Kool Herc adopted a technique used in Manhattan discothèques of working two turntables so that there was no gap when changing records. However, his groundbreaking innovation was using the two and an unsophisticated mixing board to repeat – and sample – the hottest pieces of a song to wow the crowd. This slice of the song was termed the "get-down" part, which today we call the break beats. Herc's method was to switch from turntable to turntable using a guitar amp, bouncing from channel one to channel two. He called it the "merry-go-round" technique. He watched the dance floor carefully and saw the reaction to the instrumental breaks. Herc strung all those funky breaks together, from James Brown, Incredible Bongo Band, Baby Huey, and others, creating the blueprint for hip-hop. He utilized tall public address system speakers to increase the volume without any amplifiers.

DJs took the towering speakers to parks, tennis courts, and streets and hooked into light poles to power for outdoor parties that drew breakdancers to the scene. Hip-hop became a phenomenon. In 2011, Workforce Housing Group, supported by DJ Kool Herc, took over the building and kept the apartments as affordable housing. The site is being considered for landmark status.

Address 1520 Sedgwick Avenue, Bronx, NY 10453 | Getting there Subway to East 170th Street–Grand Concourse (A, C, D train), then transfer to bus Bx18 to Sedgwick Avenue/West 174th Street | Hours Viewable from the outside only | Tip Sedgwick Avenue was renamed "Hip-Hop Boulevard" in 2016. Look for hip-hop block parties hosted at Cedar Playground, one of the places the culture grew from in the 1970s (1890 Cedar Avenue, Bronx, NY 10453, www.nycgovparks.org/parks/cedar-playground).

# 26 Crotona Park
*Home to outdoor park jams*

South of the Cross Bronx Expressway is bucolic Crotona Park, known for having the largest lake in the borough, almost 30 varieties of trees, and about 120 acres of greenery and activity space. Along with three playgrounds and a nature center, the 20 tennis courts draw a crowd. The 1888 park gets its name from Crotone, the old Italian city that produced Olympic champions in the 6th century, and so the park is designed with athletes in mind. Quiet nature walks and watching the seasons change in a park setting next to Tremont also make Crotona Park a unique destination. The park is also the spot for birdwatching with the Urban Park Rangers, SummerStage concerts, art workshops, outdoor movies, and yoga classes. But on warm-weather nights, a different energy fills the park.

The Friends of Crotona Park welcome hip-hop fans to the amphitheater, a half-moon-shaped arena spread out in a bowl overlooking the performance area. It has stone benches that are perfect for watching performances. For more than 15 years, outdoor jams have been held here to bring a wide assortment of DJs and MCs to entertain the crowds. Admission is free, but donations are accepted. The summer park jams brings b-boy and b-girl all-stars to breakdance to the music.

The Tools of War, a grassroots hip-hop association that produces the shows, was co-founded by Jorge "Fabel" Pabon (Rock Steady Crew) and Christie Z, with the idea that there are many "tools" to use in hip-hop culture: dance, microphones, paint, and turntables (@toolsofwarjams on Instagram). The group sets up turntables and throws down sheets of cardboard for breakdancing. Some of the DJs are legends from the 1970s and 1980s, a little grayer now but still up to the joy of delighting the crowd with funky beats. They're still talking about the time Grandmaster Flash (see ch. 77) dropped by and put on a blazing set.

**Address** 1700 Crotona Avenue, Bronx, NY 10457, www.nycgovparks.org/parks/crotona-park | **Getting there** Subway to 174th Street (2, 5 train) | **Hours** Daily 7am – 10pm | **Tip** Inside the park, visit the lovely Indian Lake and the former boathouse, which has been turned into a nature center and environmental education destination.

# 27 _ Denison-White House

*Historic home goes from eyesore to eyeful*

If you were asked to locate a Federal-style mansion in New York, you probably wouldn't start your search in Longwood. But there is a beautiful 19th-century house in front of the Cedars, a 2009 housing development. How a 170-year-old structure went from glamour to abandoned property to rebirth is a reason to celebrate – and visit – the Denison-White House.

In the mid-19th century, back when there were more cows than people in the South Bronx, Charles Denison, Jr. built a country house for his growing family of six. In the 1850s, the present-day Longwood area was his property. He was a successful Manhattan wholesale grocer and president of the Grocer's Bank. Upon his death, the property passed to his brother-in-law, dry goods merchant Samuel Bergh White, who used the house until his death in 1896. Developer George B. Johnson (see ch. 62) took it over as he sold houses in the neighborhood. Over the next 75 years, it was a social club, recreation center, and ultimately a neglected eyesore. It picked up a nickname, Fox Hall, for its location on Fox Street.

In the mid-1990s the crumbling walls were saved. Urban Architectural Initiatives (UAI) led the project for non-profit developers Lantern Group and Friends in the City. UAI preserved as much of the 1850s building as possible, following city landmark guidelines, to create a "green" building to minimize energy consumption. The architects used the shell of the house as a gathering site for 95 new units of affordable housing for low-income seniors and their families. The Cedars reserves apartments for generation-skipping families, or "grandfamilies," a national trend of grandparents raising grandchildren. Fox Hall has a playroom, rec center, and offices. The nine-story, $30 million project now shines in the Longwood Historic District, with one of the oldest buildings in the borough serving as the grand entrance.

Address 745 Fox Street, Bronx, NY 10455, www.thenyhc.org/projects/cedarsfox-hall |
Getting there Subway to Longwood Avenue (6 train), walk south on Southern Boulevard to
East 156th Street, make a left and walk one and a half blocks | Tip One of the most
notorious movies about the borough was *Fort Apache, The Bronx* (1981), set at the 41st Police
Precinct. A disclaimer was needed to quell New York City's unhappiness with the poor
depiction of the Bronx. The precinct relocated, and today the 1914 police station is an office
for detectives (1086 Simpson Street, Bronx, NY 10459).

# 28 Derfner Judaica Museum
*Retirement home hosts incredible art collection*

Tucked inside the Hebrew Home in Riverdale is a vibrant, small art museum and gallery that is a source of pride for the residents of this senior living center. The museum was the brainchild of Jacob Reingold, the Hebrew Home's late executive vice president, in the 1970s, and the public is invited to view a diverse collection of Jewish ceremonial art, paintings, and artifacts. According to associate curator Emily O'Leary, there are more than 4,500 pieces in the collection on every residential floor of the home's five pavilions. Paintings, mixed media, and sculpture from world-renowned and lesser-known artists are displayed. In 2009, the museum moved into a modern, light-filled facility, and today, the museum has three changing exhibitions a year and a permanent collection on view.

The Judaica collection was founded by a gift from collectors Ralph and Leuba Baum, German immigrants who escaped the Holocaust. There are objects from Jewish life and holidays, with ceremonial pieces as a core focus. Don't miss the Polish pewter menorahs, some of which are quite whimsical, and the beautiful Esther scrolls. The Baums donated a burned and tattered Torah that survived 1938's Kristallnacht in Elmshorn, a silver Seder plate, and a Sukkot plate from Hungary. As refugees from Nazi persecution, the Baums collected objects to pass on to future generations.

The outdoor sculpture gallery offers a grand, sweeping view of the Hudson River, with over 40 pieces by artists including abstract expressionist Herbert Ferber and metal sculptor Menashe Kadishman. Around the corner from the main gallery is more art by recognizable names such as Diego Rivera, Ben Shahn, and Andy Warhol. O'Leary says, "The objects are very much alive," because the residents use them for sketching and art classes, creating their own art based on what they see. The museum is free and open to the public (with photo ID). Lectures, guest speakers, and exhibition openings are available to all.

Address Palisade Avenue gate between West 261st Street and Sigma Place, Bronx, NY 10471, www.riverspringhealth.org/derfner-judaica-museum, art@hebrewhome.org | Getting there Bus Bx7, Bx10 to Riverdale Avenue / West 261st Street, walk to Palisade Avenue | Hours Sun – Thu 10:30am – 4:30pm, closed on Jewish holidays | Tip Grandparents Day was launched by Jacob Reingold at the Hebrew Home in 1961 and later became a global holiday. Annually, on the first Sunday after Labor Day, a family-friendly outdoor party and concert are held on the grounds. The event is open to the public in the sculpture garden (see website for event details).

# 29 Dutch Schultz Beer Baron

*Keeping the taps flowing during Prohibition*

There are notorious criminals, and then there was Arthur Flegenheimer, alias Dutch Schultz. Known as the Beer Baron of the South Bronx during Prohibition, he cast a long shadow over the borough. E. L. Doctorow, who grew up in the same neighborhood when Schultz ruled it, made him a central character in his novel, *Billy Bathgate*. The Bronx-born Schultz was a thief, a smuggler, and a killer. He got his start in Mott Haven, and his first speakeasy was here at 543 Brook Avenue. In a delicious twist, the building that replaced the speakeasy is now a large Fine Fare Supermarket selling 100 kinds of beer.

Around 1920, after his first stint in prison, Schultz took on his new name, apparently adopted from a dead gangster. "Flegenheimer was too long a name for headlines," he said later. Schultz brewed beer in Yonkers and kept homes and safe houses outside the New York City boundaries. He was ruthless; he's credited with more than 100 murders. A notorious bootlegger and income tax evader, he ruled the Bronx and Harlem beer market. FBI Director J. Edgar Hoover took a keen interest in catching and convicting him. Until the mid-1930s, the FBI had concerned itself with bank robbers and kidnappers, letting local law enforcement handle organized crime. Men like Schultz, Meyer Lansky, and Bugsy Siegel changed that.

New York City District Attorney Thomas Dewey was the crusader who was putting mobsters behind bars in the era. Schultz wanted to murder the D.A., but this infuriated other gangsters, who feared the heat that would bring. Lucky Luciano, of Murder Incorporated infamy, stepped in. On October 23, 1935, a gunman in a Newark restaurant attacked Schultz and four others. Schultz died the next day. Today his legend lives on in scores of books, documentaries, and true crime tours. Stop in to Fine Fare and pick up a few beers to toast Dutch Schultz.

Address 543 Brook Avenue, Bronx, NY 10455 | Getting there Subway to Third Avenue–149th Street (2, 5 train), walk two blocks east on East 149th Street | Hours Unrestricted from the outside only | Tip Celebrate the 21st Amendment at Hub Bronx Liquor & Wine, the biggest liquor warehouse in the borough. It stocks all the top brands and has steep discounts. Looking for a gallon of Henny? It's here (300 East 149th Street, Bronx, NY 10451).

# 30 East 180th Street Station

*The station that is more Venice than Van Nest*

It is incredible to believe this marvelous structure is merely an entrance to the subway system. It seems too grand, too out of place, too Italian next to the Bronx River Parkway. This is the only station in the entire system entered via a landscaped, formal plaza and passing through a landmark building on the National Register of Historic Places.

The subway stop has a rich tie to railroad commuter travel going back to its construction in 1912. It was once a station and offices for the New York, Westchester and Boston Railway Company. This railway had a brief lifespan of providing an electric train car service to the Bronx and portions of Westchester County. It connected passengers to the city's elevated train service and commuter railroads, a poor business model that generated no revenue. It went bust in 1937, and the railroad assets were liquidated. The station was taken over by the city in 1940 and used for the growing subway system.

The building was designed to look like an Italian villa by Alfred T. Fellheimer, lead architect of Grand Central Terminal and many other train stations. As the structure approached its century mark, now handling two million riders a day on the 2 and 5 lines, it needed a full modernization. For the building's centennial in 2012, the MTA invested $67 million in renovations and improvements. In 2014, the project received an Excelsior Award for Public Architecture from the New York State chapter of the American Institute of Architects.

Subway travel can be glum, but this station transports you to another realm. The plaza is grand. Look above the entrance for Mercury, the god of travelers and transporters of goods. (Mercury is also on Grand Central Terminal.) Inside, spy the new mosaics created by Luisa Caldwell, which has animals and flowers as their theme, a tribute in glass tiles to two other landmarks in the borough.

Address Intersection of East 180th Street and Morris Park Avenue, Bronx, NY 10460 |
Getting there Subway to East 180th Street (2, 5 train) | Hours Daily | Tip Go check out the
carved religious icons and statuary of St. Anthony's Roman Catholic Church. The shrine to
Our Lady of Guadalupe, also known as the Virgin of Guadalupe, is particularly beautiful
(1776 Mansion Street, Bronx, NY 10460, www.stanthonybronx.org).

# 31 _ El Fogón
## *Art space and cultural center revitalized*

Samuel Brooks, president of the Mott Haven Historic Districts Association, came to found the El Fogón Center for the Arts in a curious manner. What started as a simple business venture transformed into a vibrant, small incubator for up-and-coming local creators. "We started nine years ago," he said. "Originally my business partner Jaime Moore and I acquired the property, a bodega and the apartments above it. The space was very large, and we contemplated gutting it and putting it up for rent as another supermarket in the area. But then we made the conscious decision not to do that. We were waiting and thinking what can we do for the community. We decided to just gut the space and turn it into an alternative art space."

Brooks came to the Bronx from Honduras as a kid, graduating from South Bronx High. When he needed a name for the space, he went back to his roots. Fogón means stove or fire box, and El Fogón is named after the fire hearth, the traditional center of the Honduran kitchen. "We thought, why not call it the El Fogón Center for the Arts? The mission and vision is to be a place for young and emerging visual artists to come and exhibit their artwork, open mic events, drama performances, and it will be free of charge to them. We'll carry the maintenance and the cost associated with the space. Ultimately we wanted it to be driven by the community, where it didn't require our presence there to operate it. We managed to do that the last six or seven years with three or four individuals who run programming there. We made four keys and turned them over to four individuals to curate their own events there."

The four curators choose events for the space, which is used for everything from podcasts to art exhibitions. During any week, you might attend poetry nights, DJ sets, drumming, and live music.

Co-founders Brooks and Moore now enjoy up-and-coming artists in the space they launched.

**Address** 989 Home Street, Bronx, NY 10459, +1 (646)229-6224, www.instagram.com/
elfogon_bx | **Getting there** Subway to Freeman Street (2, 5 train), walk two blocks south
to Home and Vyse Streets | **Hours** See website for events and performances | **Tip** Comfort
food and cold drinks are served up in an historic building at Mott Haven Bar. They hold
game nights, and there's an art gallery in the back (1 Bruckner Boulevard, Bronx, NY 10454,
www.motthavenbar.com).

# 32 — Engine Co. 46 & Ladder 27
*Fighting fires since 1894*

The Fire Department (FDNY) has more than 220 firehouses across the five boroughs, and the Bronx is home to some of the oldest in the city. Many date to just after New York City consolidated in 1898, but at least one is slightly older, and is the oldest firehouse open for business in the borough. When this firehouse was dedicated in 1894 it stabled teams of horses to pull the engines and ladder trucks. For a century, big red fire apparatus roared out to protect the residents of Tremont. Today, it is home to Bronx Borough Command because the floor simply can't support heavy modern fire equipment. The FDNY uses the space for operations and planning.

Engine Company 46/Ladder 27 consists of two nearly identical buildings. They were completed in 1894 and 1904, designed by Napoleon LeBrun & Sons, the prime architecture firm of the department from 1880 to 1895. There are similar firehouses scattered throughout the city. The FDNY kept companies here until it was deemed too old for modern fire trucks.

"A lot of these old structures weren't built to hold 26,000-pound vehicles," says John Leary, fire department historian. "Sometimes it's more cost effective to just build a new firehouse and scrap the old one. But there have been many, many firehouses, like Ladder 8, the *Ghostbusters* firehouse, where they ripped out the floor, put in big I-beams, poured a new floor, and then moved the companies back in. My guess for this specific scenario for Borough Command is that they didn't need to redo the whole floor because they can park cars, which weigh a lot less than fire trucks."

Engine Company 46 / Hook and Ladder 27, nicknamed the Cross Bronx Express, moved to new quarters around the corner. While the 1975 tan brick building isn't as pretty as the old firehouse, the job for New York's Bravest remains the same today as when they drove horses to the fires.

**Address** 451-453 East 176th Street, Bronx, NY 10457, www.fdnytrucks.com/files/html/bronx/e46.htm | **Getting there** Subway to East Tremont Avenue (B, D train), walk west on Tremont two blocks to Park Avenue and make a right to East 176th Street | **Hours** Unrestricted from the outside only, but ask a firefighter for a look inside | **Tip** Big Apple Furniture & Antiques has everything from beds to vintage typewriters. You might find something as old as the firehouse (430 East 188th Street, Bronx, NY 10458).

# 33__Eugene O'Neill Movie Home

*This City Island stunner is a screen star*

In 1962, millions lined up to see the first film adaptation of Eugene O'Neill's award-winning play, *Long Day's Journey into Night*, starring Katharine Hepburn as the morphine addict Mary Tyrone. The film needed a coastal Connecticut setting, so director Sidney Lumet chose City Island's stunning 1896 Delmour's Point Mansion on Tier Street for the shoot.

Delmour's Point overlooks Eastchester Bay between City Island and the Bronx. This summer house was built for "Whispering Larry" Delmour, a Tammany Hall leader who owned stables, dairies, and real estate. He was the boss of the Upper East Side into the 1890s. Carpenter Samuel H. Booth likely both designed and built the home. The shingles, towers, and wide porch caught the public's fancy so much from passing yachts that it was a popular image on postcards. In 2000, the mansion was designated a city landmark.

O'Neill wrote the play during World War II, but it wasn't produced until 1956, three years after his death. The semi-autobiographical story was a sensation when published, and he was awarded the Pulitzer Prize posthumously.

The film starred Hepburn, Ralph Richardson, Jason Robards, and Dean Stockwell. Lumet rehearsed the cast for three weeks, and then filmed the story in the sequence of the play. *Long Day's Journey into Night* was an international hit and the cast swept the Cannes Film Festival in 1962.

City Island has a long history with movies dating back more than a century. D. W. Griffith filmed here, as did Robert De Niro in both *A Bronx Tale* and *Awakenings*. Writer-director Wes Anderson brought *The Royal Tenenbaums* to 21 Tier Street, and City Island became Eagle Island.

**Address** 21 Tier Street, Bronx, NY 10464 | **Getting there** Bus Bx29, BxM8 to City Island Avenue / Ditmars Street | **Hours** Unrestricted from the outside only | **Tip** Another house by the same builder is a short walk away, and it was named a NYC landmark in 2017. The Samuel H. and Mary T. Booth House represents "the history and development of City Island as a suburban community," the designation says (30 Center Street, Bronx, NY 10464).

# 34 The Exorcist at Fordham

*The university appears in scariest movie of all time*

Fordham is one of the most-visited college campuses for filmmakers and has been featured in scores of films including *A Bronx Tale* and *Wall Street*. It was used as a stand-in for Georgetown University for the scariest – and highest-grossing – horror film of all time, *The Exorcist*.

Despite the world of today, where horror movies have their own cable TV channel, *The Exorcist* was a sensation when it came out over the Christmas holidays (yes, it really did) in 1973. Based on the novel of the same name by William Peter Blatty, it's a fairly straightforward story about the daughter of a movie star possessed by a demon, and the battle two Catholic priests have to rid the girl of the possession. *The Exorcist* director William Friedkin won an Academy Award for his previous film, *The French Connection*, also shot on location in New York. Friedkin filmed some of the most terrifying scenes in *The Exorcist* locally, including the bedroom exorcism, in Hell's Kitchen in Manhattan.

Fordham and Georgetown are both private Jesuit-run colleges. But it was Fordham that made the movie-location money in 1972 for two crucial scenes. The Jesuit psychiatrist Father Karras (actor Jason Miller) is shown in his Georgetown room. That was shot on the fourth floor of Fordham's business school, Hughes Hall. A window was removed to accommodate a camera mounted on a crane. The scene set in a language lab was filmed in a room in the basement of Keating Hall. The same room was used as a Pentagon office in *A Beautiful Mind*.

Friedkin cast non-actors in parts in *The Exorcist*. One was a real priest, Rev. William O'Malley, S.J., who played the young priest Father Dyer. Rev. O'Malley, who taught at both Fordham Prep and Fordham, liked the experience so much that for years he screened the movie for students in Hughes Hall on the same floor where they made the movie. He retired from Fordham Prep in 2012.

**Address** 441 East Fordham Road, Bronx, NY 10458 | **Getting there** Subway to Fordham Road (B, D train); Metro-North to Fordham | **Hours** Viewable from the outside and via guided tours and open houses | **Tip** Hughes Hall is now the Gabelli School of Business. It is named for Irish immigrant John Hughes, the first Catholic archbishop of New York, founder of Fordham University (1841) and the Catholic school system (www.fordham.edu/info/20447/gabelli_school_of_business).

# 35 Father Duffy's Gravesite

*Fighting 69th chaplain lies in Old Saint Raymond's*

This seven-foot-tall granite cross marks the grave of one of the most respected figures from World War I. Father Francis Patrick Duffy served as the Catholic chaplain of the 69th Regiment, the "Fighting Irish." He was fearless in the trenches of France and earned multiple valor awards.

Father Duffy's path to becoming a legend went through the Bronx. He was born May 2, 1871 to hard-working parents in Cobourg, a Canadian mill town on Lake Ontario. Growing up poor, he worked hard at school before immigrating to America. Once in New York, he entered the seminary in Yonkers. He taught on the faculty of St. Joseph's. The church assigned him to found a new parish, Our Savior, in the Belmont section of the Bronx. Father Duffy arrived in 1912 to an empty lot and a storefront and and built the church, a school, and a nursery. But he craved more to do to serve God. He wanted to become a chaplain.

In 1914 the archdiocese appointed Father Duffy to the 69th, a New York National Guard regiment. Two years later he and the men were ordered to the US border during tensions with Mexico. Soon after returning to New York, the unit was told to prepare to ship out, and in 1917, he sailed to France with the regiment and spent all of his time in the field. He earned the reputation as the "warrior priest" for his devotion and faith. When he returned to New York he was a celebrity.

Bert Cunningham, regimental historian, calls the chaplain "a highly respected and admired religious and military hero. He should be remembered for his deep faith in God, the men of all faiths he served with great humanity, and for his love of country."

A crowd of 10,000 attended his graveside service in 1932. A sculpture of Father Duffy stands in Manhattan at Broadway and 47th Street. There was talk of moving his remains to Arlington National Cemetery; however, the Bronx was his first parish, and this is where he'll stay.

Address Old Saint Raymond's Cemetery, Puritan Avenue and East Tremont Avenue, Bronx, NY 10465, +1 (718)792-1133, www.straymondparish.org/cemetery.html, mainoffice@strayscem.com | Getting there Subway to West Farms Square – East Tremont Avenue (2 train), transfer to bus Bx40, Bx42 eastbound. Enter at Puritan Avenue and East Tremont Avenue, walk to Section 9, Range 99, Grave 10. | Hours Daily 8am–4:30pm | Tip A short walk away (Section 15, Row 19, Grave 55) is the grave of Irish immigrant Mary Mallon, best known as Typhoid Mary. Mallon (1869–1938) was a cook who infected more than 50, some fatally, before she was quarantined on North Brother Island. After her death, authorities ordered her remains cremated. The headstone you see was paid for by Mary herself.

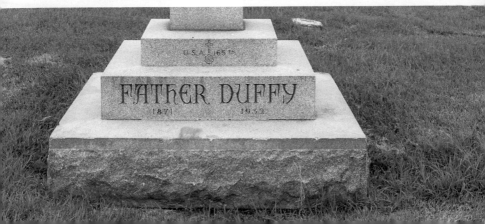

# 36___Focal Point Gallery

*Focus on photography on City Island*

For nearly half a century, Focal Point Gallery has been an institution on City Island. If you're an artist and feel your work is good enough to display on a gallery wall, bring it to proprietor Ron Terner, and he may give you an exhibit. Focal Point has multiple exhibitions throughout the year and is constantly changing the displays.

Ron has been in business for 45 years and uses the gallery as an extension of his creative life. "I grew up on Daly Avenue across from the Bronx Zoo," he says. "I went to DeWitt Clinton High and graduated with 3,000 boys – I knew almost none of them. My art background was started by watching my grandmother paint. I took classes at Lehman College for years but never graduated. I got into photography and went to the Germain School of Photography in Manhattan to learn the trade. Now everything I do is related to photography."

He came to City Island by chance. He was attending arts and crafts fairs in the early 1970s when friends introduced him to the island. "I met great people, made friends," he recalls. "I fell in love with City Island in 1974, and I'm still here."

The gallery rotates the works on exhibit on a regular basis, and Ron is always happy to provide a showcase for both new and more established artists. Almost all the exhibits have some connection to photography. Ron has student photography displayed, as well as pieces he's created over the decades. Look for Ron's bodycasts around the gallery.

To mark the gallery's 40th anniversary, Ron spent months at a rocky cove behind P.S. 175, where he created more than 70 portraits of people he'd photographed over the years who had died. Ron created memorials on the rocks for each person, a touching tribute to City Islanders who are no longer among us.

Ron follows a simple credo for the exhibits at Focal Point: "I'm looking for up-and-coming artists. No questions asked."

**Address** 321 City Island Avenue, Bronx, NY 10464, +1 (718)885-1403, www.nycgo.com/
museums-galleries/focal-point-gallery-city-island | **Getting there** Subway to Pelham Bay
Park (6 train), transfer to bus Bx29 to City Island/Fordham Street | **Hours** Mon, Wed–Sun
11am–6pm | **Tip** Johnny's Reef on the tip of the island serves meals on trays from a counter.
They specialize in fried shrimp. Go in warm weather and enjoy the waterfront views outdoors.
Cash only (2 City Island Avenue, Bronx, NY 10464, www.johnnysreefrestaurant.com).

# 37 __ Fort Number Eight

*A revolutionary relic*

On the campus of Bronx Community College in University Heights, look for Bergrisch Lecture Hall, which opened in 1964. When the foundation was being dug, a Revolutionary War fort was uncovered. A cache of army buttons and musket balls led researchers to a lost chapter in the war: the remains of Fort Number Eight, built in 1775 by colonists to protect the upper Harlem River Valley.

This section of the Bronx saw heavy activity during the war. In 1776, every able-bodied man in the city was told to help build fortifications; even servants and slaves were put to work. The series of forts that were the outer defenses to ring New York were no match for the superior numbers of the British; more than 11,000 Americans were taken as prisoners.

After the rebels were driven out, the forts were occupied by the British following their landing in 1776. Fort Number Eight was a four-sided, star-shaped fortress. It was active in the bombardment of Fort Washington in November 1776 and was the last fort controlled by the colonists in New York. The British took control of it for the duration of the war. In 1779, it was the only redcoat fort in the Bronx. The British abandoned the fort in 1782, and it was plowed over.

The history of the area wasn't forgotten. In the 19th century, Gustav H. Schwab, a steamship executive, built an estate here and named it after the fort. South Hall is his 1857 house. When the college started excavating next to the estate in the 1960s, dozens of artifacts from the war were uncovered, including somebody's 1770s dinner. The buttons and remnants of the war were given to the Bronx County Historical Society. On Signal Hill nearby is the memorial plaque about the fort. Bergrisch Hall opened almost two centuries later, and it is notable for its Marcel Breuer-designed, concrete brutalism style. The lecture hall appears to be floating over the spot where the fort once stood.

Address Northwest of West 180th Street and Sedgwick Avenue, Bronx, NY 10453, www.fortwiki.com/Fort_No._8_-_NYC | Getting there Subway to Burnside Avenue (4 train) | Hours Unrestricted | Tip University Woods south of here has fine views of the Hudson River, hiking, and is dog friendly. The three-and-a-half-acre forested park has stone walls and trails (Sedgwick Avenue and West 180th Street, Bronx, NY 10453, www.nycgovparks.org/parks/university-woods).

# 38___Frank's Sport Shop

*Everyone from pros to average joes shop here*

For nearly a century, this corner of East Tremont Avenue has drawn customers on a quest for sporting goods and apparel. Frank's Sport Shop is packed with balls, bats, cleats, equipment, and every type of uniform imaginable.

Founder Frank Stein was a Russian immigrant who passed through Ellis Island as a teenager. He worked at a Lower East Side Army-Navy store. In 1922, he moved the business to Tremont, where surplus shops proliferated. The competition welcomed him with a brick through the window. Frank persevered, and today the shop is the oldest and largest sporting goods store in the borough. Today, Frank's counts the Mets and Yankees as major accounts and is so synonymous with street fashion that the store is name-checked in songs.

Mo Stein joined his father more than 60 years ago. He has retail in his veins and likes to see his customers who walk in. "Websites are like throwing money in the sewer," Mo says. "It's like you're competing with yourself."

Frank's supplies equipment to most Major League Baseball clubs – so many players come in that Mo can't recall their names, including the time when the Mets called and asked him to keep the store open late. A limousine pulled up, and three or four ballplayers – and one of their mothers – climbed out. He does remember the day Muhammad Ali visited. The Champ showed the "rope a dope" to a group of kids.

Mo shrugs off competition from "big box stores and Fordham Road" because his staff has worked for him for decades. "We know the products," he says. "We can sell the top brands because we know them – a teenager won't." His son Ron now manages the operation. The number of hot brands that the shop carried first – or early – is lengthy. Ron curates what Frank's sells as if he were running the Met Museum Shop. "People come back here because they know what to expect," Mo says. "We never lose our customers to others."

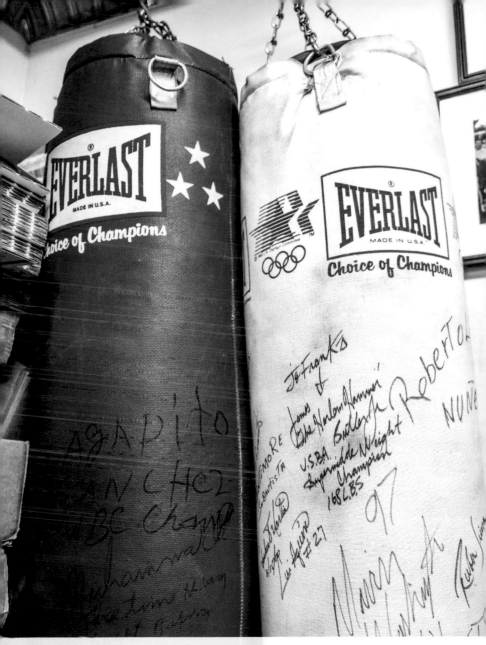

**Address** 430 East Tremont Avenue, Bronx, NY 10457, +1 (718)299-9628,
www.frankssports.com, customerservice@frankssports.com | **Getting there** Metro-North
to Tremont (Harlem Line) | **Hours** Mon–Sat 9am–8pm | **Tip** Take your new kicks and
walk three blocks to 15-acre Tremont Park, which has handball courts and baseball fields.
It recently saw a multimillion dollar renovation (Third Avenue and East Tremont Avenue,
Bronx, NY 10457, www.nycgovparks.org/parks/tremont-park).

# 39___Frankie & Johnnie's Pine

*A local institution of tasty tradition*

A 50-year-old institution for family-style Italian meals is Frankie & Johnnie's Pine Restaurant, where an ocean of *sugo all'arrabbiata* has been served up since 1969. It's been run by the Bastone family since two brothers (from a family of ten) came from Italy to set up a traditional dining experience. The sons of Frankie now oversee a large operation that has grown to a sprawling space on Bronxdale Avenue, decorated with more signed photos of New York Yankees than could ever be found in Cooperstown. Chef Frankie wears the white coat and keeps up the Calabria kitchen traditions of fresh leafy vegetables, tomatoes "from the earth," and handmade pasta he learned to make from his father. His brother, Anthony, runs the restaurant and business operations.

The menu is jammed with classic Italian fare. Chef Frankie says they want to serve up plates with "traditional food you'd want to eat with your family, and be around friendly folks. We stick with the traditional, but I do change it up a little." As the restaurant expanded, new additions were built on empty lots and neighboring properties. The dining room now seats 250, and there are many other rooms for catering and intimate dinners. In warm weather, an outdoor patio wraps around the building with a fountain, and cocktails are served al fresco.

Chef Frankie says, "I'm here since the time my father started – I was six years old. My brother is the boss. It's been a lot of good, fortunate years for us. My father really worked hard, and when we came of age, my brother took over and developed it into the place it is today."

The Pine has a long tradition of serving professional athletes; the Mets and Yankees get deliveries to the clubhouse. A steady stream of major leaguers visit; a Mets pitcher held his wedding here. The restaurant is hopping on weekend nights, as diners dig into the Calabrian-style specialties.

Address 1913 Bronxdale Avenue, Bronx, NY 10462, +1 (718)792-5956, www.fjpine.com |
Getting there Subway to Bronx Park East (2, 5 train), walk west six blocks on Rhinelander
Avenue | Hours Sun–Thu 10am–11pm, Fri & Sat 10am–midnight | Tip Bronx Park
East subway station is an elevated platform that opened in 1917 with sweeping views of the
neighborhood. The 2006 stained glass here is called "B is for Birds in the Bronx" by Candida
Alvarez (Birchall Avenue and Sagamore Street, Bronx, NY 10462).

# 40 _ Gauchos Basketball Club

*Kids from the classroom to the court*

The premier basketball academy in the city is the New York Gauchos. Established in 1967, the Gauchos annually enroll 300 boys and girls and teaches them the discipline to pursue their hoop dreams. The Gauchos claim 25 former players that made it to the NBA. Kids aged 5 – 17 fill the gym, and the spirited practices showcase the future of the sport. Weekend tournaments – open to the public – are exciting. It's inspiring to watch kids play so hard.

Tommy Swinton has been coaching here for 40 years. The Gauchos means so much to him because he gets to work with the youngest players in second and third grades. "Our mission is to help the youth in our communities," Swinton says. "We practice with the younger kids, 10 and under, on the weekends because it can be hard for them to go home after a hard practice and get their studying in. The older players don't start our first practice until 5 o'clock, but some of them get here early and do their homework upstairs before practice starts."

Homework and hard work in the classroom go hand in hand with the Gauchos. If players are not applying themselves in school, they cannot be a Gaucho. "We check report cards every quarter," Swinton says. "All the coaches check on each player on their team. 90 – 95 percent of the girls go to college. On our high school team, about 95 – 97 percent of the kids go on to play on college teams."

The Gauchos return to the gym often, even the ones who made it to the NBA. "They always come back and say thank you for the work that you've done, and that feels good," Swinton says. "They don't always understand the work you put in when they were younger, but in the end, they respect the program. They're happy with what we've done for them. Our kids always come through and show love. Stephon Marbury came in last week – he just stopped by to say hello when he was in town. We get that all the time."

**Address** 478 Gerard Avenue, Bronx, NY 10451, +1 (718)665-6952, www.newyorkgauchos.org | **Getting there** Subway to 149th Street–Grand Concourse (2, 4, 5 train) | **Hours** Check website for tournament schedule | **Tip** Hit the streets with the Boogie Down Bronx Runners. This running crew is open to all. Follow @boogiedownbronxrunners on Instagram for updates. They host a free 5K group run every Tuesday at 7pm from the Pelham Cornerstone Community Center (785 Pelham Parkway North, Bronx, NY 10467).

# 41___Ghost of Pelham Bay Park
## *The Native American girl who saved the Revolution*

The rich history in the Bronx means that there is no shortage of stories about haunted spots in the borough. The Stockbridge Indians are said to haunt Van Cortlandt Park (see ch. 97). Van Cortlandt House Museum isn't only the oldest house in the borough (see ch. 101), it's also the oldest haunted house in the Bronx. Dolls are said to move around on their own, voices whisper from other realms, and even singing has been heard. Looking for ghosts is part of the experience when you go on the guided tours.

Siwoney Trail is an especially good place to get scared. Go for a nice hike in Pelham Bay Park, and you might hear running feet – but not from anyone wearing Nikes. The legend goes that these steps date back to the year that the Founding Fathers signed the Declaration of Independence. A Native American girl, running in what is today nearby Orchard Beach, warned the Americans that British ships led by General William Howe were approaching Pelham Bay from the South (see ch. 11). The brave girl's warning was given to rebel forces and allowed General George Washington enough advance warning to escape the vicinity. Without this crucial information, the British might have defeated the Americans that day. Mysterious sounds of the girl's footfalls are said to be heard in quiet places in the park today.

Fordham University is the most haunted school in the borough. An 18th-century hospital and Rose Hill Manor once occupied the grounds. Students and staff have been reporting paranormal activity for generations, and the spooky underground tunnels that connect some school buildings only fuel the legends. A relatively new ghost is a worker who died while building O'Hare Hall in 2000. He is said to bang on walls and stroll the halls. With nearly 600 students in the building, the story gets repeated often. The school's tie to *The Exorcist* (see ch. 34) is the icing on the cake.

Address Watt Avenue and Middletown Road, Bronx, NY 10465, www.nycgovparks.org/ parks/pelham-bay park | Getting there Subway to Pelham Bay Park (6 train), transfer to bus Bx5, Bx12 (summer only, check MTA schedule) | Hours Daily 10am – 6pm | Tip While immortal silent screen star Olive Thomas is said to haunt the Ziegfeld Theatre in Times Square – where she was a Follies Girl in 1915 – she does not haunt her grave. Thomas lies in a forlorn mausoleum in Woodlawn, where her ghost has never been spotted (4199 Webster Avenue, Bronx, NY 10470, www.thewoodlawncemetery.org).

# 42 Great War Memorial Grove

*Hundreds of trees represent lives lost*

Tree memorials in public spaces function to recall lives lost so that the dead are not forgotten. Memorial groves – stands of trees planted together – serve as focal points for remembrance ceremonies. A tree stands for a lost person, but taken together they show a natural progression of time and the passing of seasons. One of the largest memorial groves on the East Coast, perhaps in the United States, stands in Pelham Bay Park. It is part of the Bronx County War Memorial, a two-part memorial on Shore Road that honors 950 Bronxites who gave their lives during World War I.

The American Legion planted tree memorials along the Grand Concourse in 1921, but seven years later, a subway expansion necessitated that the trees be moved, and they were brought here to create a memorial grove. Several hundred maple and linden trees were planted in rows across 32 acres to approximate a military cemetery. There are no markers on the trees, so they are not easy to identify.

Architect John J. Sheridan, a captain in the war, designed the monument. *Winged Victory* and the limestone reliefs were a collaboration between the husband and wife team of Belle Kinney, a native of Tennessee, and Leopold Scholz, a prize-winning graduate of the Imperial Academy of Fine Arts in Vienna. *Victory* weighs 7,300 pounds and stands atop a column of 14 discs; the overall height of the monument is 120 feet. The memorial was unveiled September 24, 1933, for a crowd of more than 150,000 residents, including Gold Star mothers. It has the names of 947 local soldiers lost. When the statue was dedicated, 947 white doves were released. Eventually the memorial fell victim to the elements, neglect, and vandalism, but the Parks Department restored the monument and repaired the sculpture at a cost of more than $1 million. It was rededicated on Veterans Day 2001.

Address Shore Road, Pelham Bay Park, Bronx, NY 10465, www.nycgovparks.org/parks/
pelham-bay-park | Getting there Subway to Pelham Bay Park (6 train), walk northeast on
Shore Road | Hours Daily 6am–10pm | Tip Behind the memorial are wonderful hiking
trails that lead to the bay and Orchard Beach (www.nycgovparks.org/parks/pelham-bay-
park/facilities/hikingtrails).

# 43__Growing Up E. L. Doctorow

*Childhood home of the famous novelist*

The greatest novelist to come out of the Bronx was Edgar Lawrence "E. L." Doctorow, born in 1931, who grew up during the Depression and watched the borough transformed by immigration. His childhood memories play a major role in his novels, columns, and stories. Doctorow was a graduate of the Bronx High School of Science, and his love for the Bronx never dimmed. In 2013, he wrote of his neighborhood, "This part of the Bronx, new and open under the sky, had flourished in the few years since the independent subway line had been extended from Manhattan, making possible a fast commute into town. This was the faux-rural Borough of Escape for all the folks working their way out of the Lower East Side. And it was an equitable society, everyone penniless together, scraping along."

He lived mere blocks from Bathgate Avenue, which he used as the name for the protagonist of his award-winning novel, *Billy Bathgate*. The coming-of-age story puts Billy into the inner circle of the iconic Bronx gangster Dutch Schultz (see ch. 29), becoming part of his gang and witness to the Dutchman's crimes. Doctorow created a gun-toting Holden Caulfield character from his own neighborhood. The homes, streets, and parks around Bathgate Avenue add color to the gritty novel.

Doctorow was awarded every major literary award for his fiction, and was inducted into the New York State Writers Hall of Fame on the basis of his Bronx roots and success in capturing his hometown on the page. In 2012 he was awarded the PEN Saul Bellow Award given to an author whose "scale of achievement over a sustained career places him in the highest rank of American Literature." His tidy two-story childhood home, where he resided in 1940, is still standing and isn't changed much. The empty lot next door would be perfect for a literary museum.

Address 1658 Eastburn Avenue, Bronx, NY 10457 | Getting there Subway to
174th-175th Street (B, D train), walk south on Morris Avenue to Eastburn Avenue |
Hours Unrestricted from the outside only | Tip Always a Bronx boy, Doctorow came
home. Visit his gravesite, with a gravestone in the shape of a book, at Woodlawn
Cemetery. He is mere feet from Herman Melville (3800 Jerome Avenue, Bronx,
NY 10467, www.thewoodlawncemetery.org).

# 44 Hall of Fame for Great Americans

*This is the hall that started them all*

Decades before Cooperstown and its heroes of the diamond, or Cleveland's shrine to rock gods, there was the Hall of Fame for Great Americans. At one time it was front-page news when members were inducted. Today only when members are removed does it get attention.

The roots of the hall go back to the 19th century when New York University moved its campus from Washington Square to a lush campus overlooking the Hudson. Chancellor Henry M. MacCracken dreamed up the hall and created an electoral college of great minds from across the nation to choose inductees. Stanford White designed the 630-foot-long open-air limestone and granite colonnade.

The first class was inducted in 1900. Because fame can be fleeting, members must be deceased for at least 25 years. The 104 include Founding Fathers, presidents, and inventors. It's light on women and minorities. It's interesting to think of who ought to be members.

The usual suspects such as Samuel Clemens, Ralph Waldo Emerson, and the Wright Brothers take their places next to men and women you'll need look up. These are the white male ministers, preachers, and theologians. The top sculptors of the era worked on the busts – look for examples by Daniel Chester French (Edgar Allan Poe) and Augustus Saint-Gaudens (Abraham Lincoln). Controversy swirled recently when Confederate Hall of Famers were removed; find the empty niches of Robert E. Lee and Stonewall Jackson.

Seventy years after opening, NYU went broke, sold off the campus, and returned to Manhattan. Today Bronx Community College operates here. The hall hasn't elected any new members since the 1970s, so no busts have been added in nearly 50 years. However, it's nice to know there is such a Hall of Fame, and at one time, it was the only one in the nation.

**Address** Sedgwick Avenue and Hall of Fame Terrace, Bronx, NY 10453, +1 (718)289-5100,
www.bcc.cuny.edu/about-bcc/history-architecture/hall-of-fame | **Getting there** Subway to
Burnside Avenue (4 train). Walk west on Burnside for four blocks to University Avenue.
Make a right and walk one and a half blocks north on University Avenue to campus gates.
Visitors must present photo ID to campus security guards, who will direct you to the Hall
of Fame. | **Hours** Daily 9am–5pm, Sat & Sun 10am–4pm | **Tip** Walk next door to explore
Gould Memorial Library, a stunning 1899 example of Stanford White's most opulent
designs. The building is decayed, but it remains an architectural marvel to behold. In 2012
it was named a National Landmark (Sedgwick Avenue and Hall of Fame Terrace, Bronx,
NY 10453, www.bcc.cuny.edu/about-bcc/history-architecture/gould-memorial-library).

# 45 Henry Hudson Monument

*English explorer honored in grand gesture*

To celebrate the 300th anniversary of Henry Hudson's sailing to North America and 100th anniversary of Robert Fulton's first steamboat, New York pulled out all the stops in 1909. Parties, parades, and gala events were held across the city. Wilbur Wright was hired to fly over the river, the very first time an airplane flew over the city – or actually over water. The Navy sent warships up the Hudson. Hundreds dined at a splashy banquet at the Hotel Astor in Times Square. But today, only the Bronx, which abuts the river bearing Hudson's name, has a monument and park to recall the grand festivities. The imposing figure high above the treetops – visible to all drivers on the Henry Hudson Parkway – has a quirky back story.

For the tercentenary, a sculpture of the explorer atop a pedestal was commissioned in 1906. Sculptor Karl Bitter got the job. He made a plaster maquette of Hudson in time for the celebration, with his hands at his sides, his body positioned as to be looking towards a distant shore. In 1912, the architectural firm of Babb, Cook and Welch designed the 100-foot-high Doric column, which was placed in the park. This is as far as the project ever went. Bitter was tragically killed in 1915 when a car struck him. Funds for the sculpture dried up. The column stood for 26 years without Hudson atop it.

In 1935, Parks Commissioner Robert Moses took action to rectify the sorry state of the memorial. When a new bridge linking the Inwood district of Manhattan with Spuyten Duyvil in the Bronx was planned, the park and monument got new attention. The location is perfect: while sailing on the river that would one day carry his name, Hudson sought shelter in Spuyten Duyvil Creek. A student of Bitter's, sculptor Karl H. Gruppe, finished the job. In 1938, the captain of the *Halve Maen* (Half Moon) could finally look over the river that bears his name.

Address Independence Avenue and West 227th Street, Bronx, NY 10463, www.nycgovparks.org/parks/henry-hudson-park/highlights/11789 | Getting there Bus Bx10, Bx20, BxM1, BxM2 to Henry Hudson Parkway East/West 227th Street | Hours Daily 6am–10pm | Tip Some of the most beautiful local apartments inspired by Italian villas are inside the aptly named Villa Charlotte Bronte, located in Spuyten Duyvil. Built in 1927, these 17 apartments are perched overlooking the river and appear more Borgia than Bronx. Take note of the arches and walkways of these stunning homes (2501 Palisade Avenue, Bronx, NY 10463).

# 46__Heritage Collection
*Culture kept alive in the stacks*

One of the gems of the borough is the Bronx Library Center, which, in addition to being a public library, contains the deep Latino & Puerto Rican Heritage Collection and Gallery. There is a special collection housed here that offers free exhibitions and space for researchers to explore Puerto Rican culture and history. On the fourth floor is a modest room that is home to over 800 academic titles, biographies, histories, literature, poetry, and photography books. The collection includes *Actas de Congreso Internacional de Julia de Burgos*, *Arte Latino Americano*, the *Grand Encyclopedia of Puerto Rico*, slim books of poems, and heritage collections. Ask a librarian to let you inside.

The small center has touches of Puerto Rico throughout, from the framed photos to the decor. A basket of musical instruments, a wellworn set of dominos, native pinecones, and red and blue flowers remind visitors of the island. On a wall hangs a family tapestry from the Tomas and Modesta Arte descendants, a quilt of T-shirts made over the years from island family reunions. A quote from Psalm 78:6 can speak for this entire collection: "So the next generation would know them, even the children yet to be born and they in turn would tell their children."

National Hispanic Heritage Month runs from September 15 to October 15. The library hosts events including an ancestry workshop, art lessons, and screenings.

Opened in 2006, the Bronx Library Center is the first green building built for New York City. It has six floors to serve the community, and an outreach and education program that focuses on the needs of the changing neighborhood. It is the largest public library in the Bronx. The library hosts weekly book discussions, film screenings, performances, and talks. In warm weather check out the outdoor reading terrace on the roof, six stories above the treetops. You can see for miles.

**Address** 310 East Kingsbridge Road, Bronx, NY 10458, +1 (718)579-4244, www.nypl.org/blc | **Getting there** Subway to Fordham Road (B, D train), walk four blocks northwest | **Hours** Mon–Sat 9am–9pm, Sun noon–6pm | **Tip** Imitation is the sincerest form of flattery because the Bronx has its own Flatiron Building. Designed by builder-owner Otto Schwarzler in the 1920s, this building's tall, narrow corner inspires comparison to its world-famous close cousin in Manhattan (1882 Grand Concourse, Bronx, NY 10457).

# 47 Heritage Field

*Walk around where legends roamed*

The park across the street from Yankee Stadium is the former location of The House That Ruth Built. From 1923 to 2008, it was the home of the Yankees until it was razed for a 21st-century upgrade. When the old ballpark was leveled, the land was swapped with the city to use for Macombs Dam Park. It is now possible to run around the field where Yogi Berra, Lou Gehrig, Reggie Jackson, Joltin' Joe DiMaggio, and hundreds of other Hall of Fame players once played America's pastime.

Don't show up with your friends and expect a pickup game of baseball. This isn't like *Field of Dreams*, and Shoeless Joe Jackson isn't coming out of the bushes. Because it's a city park, you need a permit to play ball here, but it's fairly easy to find an open gate someplace on the fence to walk in and stroll around. The old basepaths and location of home plate are not easily found. If they were once marked it's now a challenge to figure out exactly where Mickey Mantle and Roger Maris smashed home runs from. Heritage Field's southern ball field is aligned with the original Stadium's footprint and is roughly in the same place. When games are underway across the street, it's possible to hear the roar of the crowd from here.

If Heritage Field doesn't mean much to non-baseball fans, this spot holds other cachet. Love football history? This is where coach Knute Rockne said, "Win one for the Gipper" to his Notre Dame team in 1928, and 30 years later where the Colts beat the Giants for the NFL championship in the "Greatest Game Ever Played." Boxing matches, concerts by Pink Floyd and U2, and multiple visits by the Pope all happened here. This is also a good place for a run, and the track around the park gets a lot of people pounding the pavement. The field itself is patchy and not kept up and manicured like it was when Derek Jeter patrolled the infield. However, this is the best place for a selfie, no matter what team you root for.

Address River Avenue and East 161st Street, Bronx, NY 10451 | Getting there Subway to 161st Street–Yankee Stadium (4, D train) | Hours Daytime only | Tip Walk across the street to new Yankee Stadium. The club offers tours of the ballpark, with a trip to the field, small museum, and clubhouse included (1 East 161st Street, Bronx, NY 10451, www.mlb.com/yankees/ballpark/tours).

# 48__The High Bridge
*A tall landmark reopened above the Harlem River*

The oldest bridge in New York City closed when The Beatles were still together and didn't reopen until 2015. Restoring public access to the High Bridge was a shot in the arm for the Bronx and Manhattan, and unlike Manhattan's High Line, there are beautiful natural views. The 140-foot-tall (43 meters) bridge opened in 1848 and was originally named Aqueduct Bridge. It was a pedestrian walkway until it succumbed to vandalism and poor maintenance and closed. New York City Department of Parks and Recreation restored and renovated the national historic landmark, which connects Highbridge in the Bronx to Washington Heights in Manhattan.

Its history is tied to a thirsty city. Manhattan was booming, but there wasn't enough water. The city tapped a source 40 miles away in Westchester County and built this brick and stone aqueduct, an engineering marvel, to pipe water south to Manhattan. Rising over the Harlem River, the High Bridge was a key part of the Croton Aqueduct, with 15 masonry arches designed by engineer John B. Jervis. In 1928, to the dismay of the public, five arches were removed and replaced by an ugly steel section. The bridge was a popular destination for walkers, including Bronx resident Edgar Allan Poe (see ch. 104), to enjoy the views and watch boat races. Today it reconnects the two boroughs and is the perfect spot to indulge in a selfie or two.

Lesley Walter, Vice President of Friends of the Old Croton Aqueduct, leads tours of the High Bridge. "I get a lot of people from below Central Park and Westchester, and it's eye-opening to them," she says. Walter points out that the bridge is not just scenic. "The bridge is functional, opening a gateway for this part of New York City and also connecting families on both sides of the river. This bridge is opening up the area to the rest of New York State; it's exciting to take people up there."

**Address** University Avenue and West 170th Street, Bronx, NY 10452, www.nycgovparks.org/park-features/highbridge-park/planyc | **Getting there** Subway to 170th Street (4 train), walk to East 170th Street and turn left to the park | **Hours** Daily 7am–7pm, closes earlier in winter | **Tip** Friends of the Old Croton Aqueduct offers walking tours of the bridge, trail, and neighborhood. They also are advocates who clean up the trail and organize events (www.aqueduct.org).

# 49 Home of the Needle Drop

*Birthplace of a DJ style*

The five-story apartment house built in 1900 looks like a lot of others in the area. But it's unique. This is where a junior high school student and his mother's record player set the course for every DJ who ever held the needle over a spinning disc of vinyl and waited to drop it. Theodore Livingston was a student at Morris High when he invented two of the core components of hip-hop: scratching and the "needle drop." As his fame grew, he was reborn as Grand Wizzard Theodore.

"I was 12 years old and practicing in my mom's house," Livingston recalled. "I came home from school and wanted to make a mix tape. During the course of doing that, I created the scratch. The music we practiced was in my mom's house, so obviously we had to go by her rules. So I was in the house and being so loud when she came in the room and told me to turn the music down or cut the music off – those few seconds would seem like an eternity. That's when I created the scratch."

Watching the vinyl rotate on the turntable, he observed the grooves carefully, detecting the pattern of where the "break" in the track was. "If you spend a lot of time with vinyl and looking at the vinyl, you're able to read the record," Livingstone said. "You can see the dark lines, which are the end of one song and the beginning of the next. You can be in the middle of one record and see the darkest part, and that will be the break part. So you can pick the needle up and get it to the break part – it might be at the beginning, at the middle, or the end of the record – but once you spend a lot of time with the record, you get to know where the breaks are."

Now he teaches DJs at Jam Master Jay's Scratch Academy and tours around the world. "I travel around to schools and colleges and talk about my life as a DJ and the early days of hip-hop," Livingston says. His old home is part of the story.

Address 1199 Boston Road, Bronx, NY 10456, www.facebook.com/theodorelivingston |
Getting there Subway to Freeman Street (2, 5 train), walk west on Freeman Street, turn right
onto East 169 Street. Turn left onto Boston Street and walk one block. | Hours Unrestricted
from the outside only | Tip Jackson Forest Community Garden is a 9,000-square-foot space
in Claremont Village. GrowNYC rebuilt the gardens in 2017, building raised beds and picnic
tables (722 Home Street, Bronx, NY 10456, www.grownyc.org/gardens/bx/jackson-forest-
community-garden).

# 50   Hostos Center for the Arts
*Variety of arts on display*

Out of the dark days of the South Bronx grew a college, and from that seed bloomed an arts center, which has blossomed into a vibrant neighborhood destination for art, dance, drama, and music. This is Hostos Center for the Arts & Culture on the campus of Hostos Community College. It is approaching four decades of diverse programming. The concerts, lectures, shows, and workshops are open to the community and bring artists from around the world to the center. The centerpiece is an art gallery, a 367-seat theater, and a 907-seat concert hall.

The college was founded in 1968 and is named for Eugenio Maria de Hostos (1839–1903), the author, educator, and orator who was born in Puerto Rico. The roots of the arts center go back to 1982, when the college used a portable stage in a Grand Concourse gymnasium to present concerts and exhibitions. At the time the school was working on building its image, as it transitioned from offering a limited number of degrees to the broad-based programs it's know for today. The multimillion dollar arts and culture center opened in 1994 and has since become an important part of the South Bronx community.

It offers a stellar roster of events focused on Latino culture. With the three venues in the center, audiences have their pick of events in multiple disciplines: dance, film, lectures, and music. There is a large amount of children's programming aimed at those under 12. Longwood Art Gallery, with polished white floors and walls, museum-quality design, and natural light, looks like it was transported from Chelsea. The Bronx Council on the Arts curates group shows featuring artists from the borough, giving them valuable exposure.

The repertory theater offers a wide range of performances. Musicians from around the world bring one-night shows, dancers bring ballet, and festivals program days-long special events.

Address 450 Grand Concourse, Bronx, NY 10451, +1 (718)518-4455, www.hostos.cuny.edu/culturearts | Getting there Subway 139th Street–Grand Concourse (2, 4, 5 train) | Hours See website for schedule | Tip Movies on the rooftop of Bronx Terminal Market are offered in the summer. Bring a lawn chair and picnic blanket for the sunset show (610 Exterior Street, Bronx, NY 10451, www.bronxterminalmarket.com).

# 51__Jack's Bait and Tackle

*Before dropping a line, drop by the shop*

With fishing poles galore and buckets of bait, everything you need to catch a whopper is under one roof at Jack's Bait and Tackle, the oldest family-owned marine supply store in the Bronx. A third-generation family business on City Island, Jack's is the spot for everything from bait to foul-weather gear. A World War II US Marine veteran launched the business. Today it's run by his grandson, and is one of the largest wholesalers of bait on the East Coast.

Enter the long and narrow shop on City Island Avenue, and you are entering the wide world of fishing. It stocks hooks and rods for reeling in any type of underwater creature. This is the supply spot for local anglers, from sport fishermen to those who are putting dinner on the table. New York City is surrounded by water, and there are plenty of places for fishing. Bridge abutments, dock pilings, rocky jetties, and other man-made structures are hiding places for many varieties of fish. With so many different bodies of water within a short boat trip from City Island, the boundaries around the city are perfect for catching seasonal species. New York Department of Environmental Conservation (www.dec.ny.gov) sponsors Free Fishing Days, where licenses aren't required, and City Island is a key destination.

The big charter boats that venture past Montauk Point, the deep saltwater fisherman needs to be better prepared with heavy lines and more expensive rods and reels. Party boats with 100 fishermen packed aboard pile through to stock up on bait before heading out. Sandworms and clams are popular for catching porgies and striped bass.

The store is busiest from March through December. Before sunrise, fishermen line up to board their boats, fresh bait from Jack's in their coolers. Some of the best fishing on the East Coast is within a short distance from City Island. Hooking striped bass in Jamaica Bay alongside the JFK runways is something locals look forward to. For more than 70 years Jack's has been that go-to store for fishing supplies.

**Address** 551 City Island Avenue, Bronx, NY 10464, +1 (718)885-2042, www.jacksbaitandtackle.com | **Getting there** Subway to Pelham Bay Park (6 train), transfer to bus Bx29 to City Island Avenue/Cross Street | **Hours** Daily 8am–6pm | **Tip** Charter a boat, small or large, or find a City Island captain by using the Chamber of Commerce, which maintains a directory of all local captains who are members (www.cityislandchamber.org).

# 52___Jake LaMotta's Bronx

*Where the Raging Bull took his gloves off*

The hard-punching boxer Jake LaMotta was brought to the Bronx as a child when his immigrant parents moved to the borough from the Lower East Side of Manhattan. He showed early promise as a boxer, and his father made him fight neighborhood kids for rent money.

LaMotta got his start at local club fights in the West Farms neighborhood. These were held in the New York Coliseum, popularly called the Bronx Coliseum, on East 177th Street, which was used for boxing, circuses, hockey, and music. It became the West Farms Bus Depot before it was demolished.

Known as a brutal fighter, the middleweight was nicknamed the Bronx Bull. Among his mottos was, "Fear is unnecessary." LaMotta threw a fight on November 14, 1947 at Madison Square Garden. The match was run by mobster Frankie Carbo of the Lucchese crime family. He told LaMotta he would have to take a dive if he wanted a crack at the title. However, the match was so obviously fixed that the state boxing commission held up the purse, launched an investigation, and suspended LaMotta. Once reinstated, he fought his way to become the World Middleweight Champion in 1949.

LaMotta compiled a record of 83 wins, 19 losses, and 4 draws. He had 30 wins by way of knockout, and was the first man to beat Sugar Ray Robinson. They went on to have a legendary six-bout rivalry. On February 14, 1951, Robinson won by a TKO in the 13th round. The fight was stopped with LaMotta hanging on the ropes.

During part of his time in the Bronx, this great athlete lived in the Morris Park neighborhood at 994 Neill Avenue, a tidy two-story on a corner lot with a small backyard and shade trees. LaMotta lived to 95 and died in 2017.

"I was able to convince my body that I could take it and nobody could hurt me," LaMotta said. "I might've gotten cut, stitches over my eyes. Broken nose. Broken hands. But I never really got hurt."

**Address** 994 Neill Avenue, Bronx, NY 10462 | **Getting there** Subway to Morris Park (5 train), walk two blocks south on Colden Avenue | **Hours** Unrestricted from the outside only | **Tip** Have cocktails and shoot some pool like Jake would at the spacious Park Billiards sports bar, a casual local institution that boasts a full bar and tasty appetizers (2020 White Plains Road, Bronx, NY 10462, www.parkbilliards.com).

# 53__Joe's Place

*All the comforts of a Puerto Rican kitchen*

One of the most beloved chefs in the borough is waiting to serve you juicy *mechado* that will make you feel like you're in Puerto Rico. Joe Torres has cooked for everyone from Derek Jeter to Jennifer Lopez, and now he runs an inviting family restaurant in the shadow of the Number 6 train in Parkchester. Joe's Place is the culmination of a long life spent in busy kitchens.

"I came here from Guaynabo at 9 and started cooking at 14," Joe says. "My mother taught me how to cook. I worked in Manhattan hotels and restaurants as a teenager. Daytime I was at the old Americana Hotel. Then I'd go over to the Cattleman on 45th Street and work at night. I was there 18 years."

Joe worked so many long hours that when his friends were riding the subway, he was driving a big Cadillac. He spent decades cooking steaks in Manhattan until he got a call that changed everything. Jimmy Rodriguez opened his restaurant-nightclub Jimmy's Bronx Cafe on Fordham Road in 1993. Joe would be the chef. For a decade, it was the destination for Yankees, musicians, models, and politicians. "I fed Fidel Castro roast pork," Joe said. "Security was all over the place, and I couldn't get close to him."

"Jimmy liked for me to come out in my 'big white hat' and meet people," Joe recalled. So he transformed him from the guy in the kitchen to the chef everyone wanted to know. He knew he wanted to open his own place eventually. "I wanted to do something with food and be proud of it as a Puerto Rican, and stick to my roots. I love rice and beans!"

Joe's Place is the restaurant he always wanted. "Now it's been more than 20 years cooking Caribbean food," Joe says. "Our *mechado* is a very good-looking dish. Cow feet soup is a traditional Spanish dish. Try the *mofongo* stuffed with shrimp, or sweet plantains and yuca. For dessert get the *tembleque* – it's cocoa based." Everyone is welcome.

Address 1841 Westchester Avenue, Bronx, NY 10472, +1 (718)918-2947, www.joesplacebronx.com | Getting there Subway to Parkchester (6 train), walk three blocks west to Westchester and Thieriot Avenues | Hours Daily 8am–midnight | Tip On Virginia Avenue, look for street art of strong Bronx women by graffiti artists Laura Alvarez and Karen Pedrosa (1281-1255 Virginia Avenue, Bronx, NY 10472, www.bx200.com/portfolio/laura-alvarez, www.karenpedrosa.com).

# 54__Jolly Tinker

*Down the hatch is in order*

The tiny bar cannot be missed from the outside: it is painted canary yellow with green trim. A longtime hangout for Fordham undergrads and workers from the New York Botanical Garden, the Jolly Tinker is a quiet spot by day and a raucous gathering place late nights. Turning 50, the Jolly Tinker is one of the oldest bars in the borough, which is a point of pride for the new owners.

Once, Bedford Park and Belmont claimed a collection of Irish pubs. In 1969, the Tinker was opened by an immigrant from County Waterford, and the family famously never closed for a single day for 48 years of ownership. New owners arrived in 2017, and the Irish flag, framed pictures, and vintage memorabilia were carted out. However, the bar still carries on the name from the Clancy Brothers song:

*The missus came out to the door and she asked me to come in*
*"You're welcome jolly tinker and I hope you brought your tin"*
*Well indeed I did, don't you know I did.*

The new owners completely renovated the bar. The menu is all bar fare and comfort food, offering tasty clams, a variety of seafood, and crispy wings. The Tinker Burger is piled high with American cheese. The bar also has a full cocktail menu, with frozen drinks as a specialty. The Tinker is split into two sections: the bar is on the first floor, and the dining room is next door, accessible via a stairway alongside the bar. There are DJs playing hip-hop, trap, Latin, and R&B. Live music and dancing on the weekends is popular. Check the website for the regular events schedule and lineup of performers and DJ nights. The interior is minimally decorated, but there are two aquariums with a couple of extremely languorous fish who swim unfazed by the commotion around them. The pool table is a popular spot in the evenings.

When you reach the corner of Bedford Park Boulevard and Webster Avenue, you can't miss the Jolly Tinker's yellow building.

**Address** 2875 Webster Avenue, Bronx, NY 10458, +1 (347)726-5644, www.jollytinkers.com, jollytinker@jollytinkers.com | **Getting there** Subway to Bedford Park Boulevard (B, D train), walk south 0.4 mile on Bedford Park Boulevard | **Hours** Mon–Sat 11–4am, Sun noon–4am | **Tip** A classic diner of the old-school variety is Webster Cafe & Diner. It's known for welcoming families with kids and is close to the Bronx Zoo and the New York Botanical Garden (2873 Webster Avenue, Bronx, NY 10458, www.webstercafenyc.com).

# 55 Kingsbridge Armory

*No roof is bigger than this one*

The Kingsbridge Armory holds the record as the largest armory in the world. At one time, armories were important parts of communities, and all five boroughs had them. Following the Civil War, men joined local regiments for regular drills, and in World War I, the National Guard used the spaces. After the war, the units shrank in size again, and these massive imposing structures became obsolete. Such was the fate of the Kingsbridge Armory, built between 1912 and 1917 for the Eighth Coastal Artillery Regiment, which had the honor of escorting George Washington to the first presidential inauguration, earning its nickname, the "Washington Greys." The size of the building is staggering. The armory occupies almost the entire five-acre block between West Kingsbridge Road, Jerome Avenue, West 195th Street, and Reservoir Avenue.

The façade along Kingsbridge Road is a Romanesque-style fortress built to look like a medieval fort, with towers more Lord of the Rings than any kind of military installation. This side houses the administrative portion, and behind it lies that incredible roof. The most notable feature is the 180,000-square-foot drill hall, 120-foot high with a double-truss ceiling. It's so big that artillery shells could be safely fired indoors.

When the armory first opened, it had a dirt floor, and soldiers set up tents and dug trenches. Over the decades, the National Guard used the building for every conflict from World War I to the Cold War. When the troops were away, the building was rented to pay the bills. It hosted bike races, shows for boaters and dog breeders, and moviemaking. In the 1950s, kids were invited to climb on tanks and ride an observation balloon indoors.

The military moved out in 1996, and the armory was nearly converted into a mall. Solid plans are underway to turn the site into a national ice skating center, with nine ice rinks operating year round.

Address 29 West Kingsbridge Road, Bronx, NY 10468 | Getting there Subway to Kingsbridge Road (4 train) | Hours Unrestricted from the outside only | Tip Director Martin Scorsese filmed *The Irishman* with Robert De Niro at the nearby American Legion Post 774 (3035 Corlear Avenue, Bronx, NY 10463).

# 56 Kips Bay Boys & Girls Club

*Launching pad for Jenny from the block*

The biggest modern star who hails from the Bronx is Jennifer Lopez (JLo), who grew up in Castle Hill. Before the platinum records and movies, Lopez was a schoolgirl with a dream of seeing her name in lights. After school, she would go to the local Boys & Girls Club, where she would have the chance to act, dance, and sing. This club played a key role in the development of her career in entertainment. Lopez's talent, dedication, and hard work paid off, as she became the most recognizable Latin performer in the US – and it all started at this neighborhood youth center.

Lopez was born in Castle Hill and lived with her parents and siblings in apartments before moving to a house at 2210 Blackrock Avenue, where she lived until age 16. The "block" from her hit single is the corner around Castle Hill and Blackrock Avenues. She attended nearby Holy Family School (2169 Blackrock Avenue) where her mother Guadalupe taught kindergarten. Lopez graduated from Preston High in Throgs Neck. She spent time after school at the Kips Bay Boys & Girls Club in the performing arts program. When Lopez released her third studio album *This Is Me… Then*, she went back to the club. Lopez continues to return and give back: proceeds from her first-ever Bronx concert, at Orchard Beach in 2014, went to the club.

Her breakout debut album *On the 6* is also a nod to her roots. Anyone who has ever waited on the 6 train to travel from one world in the Bronx to another in Manhattan can relate to that song. While she has a star on Hollywood Boulevard and a shelf of awards, Lopez is also a member of the Boys & Girls Clubs of America Alumni Hall of Fame. "When I was a little girl from the Bronx running to Kips Bay Boys & Girls Club to sing and dance…I didn't know what was in store for me then," she said. "But I know that with Kips Bay Boys & Girls Club, I had a place to go."

**Address** 1930 Randall Avenue, Bronx, NY 10473, www.kipsbay.org | **Getting there** Subway to Parkchester (6 train), transfer to bus Bx39 on White Plains Road to Randall Avenue | **Hours** See website for hours and events | **Tip** Actress and *Scandal* star Kerry Washington also is a club alumnus, and JLo once taught her to dance. Washington was raised in the Jamie Towers in Soundview (633 Olmstead Avenue, Bronx, NY 10473).

LUCILE PALMARO CLUBHOUSE

# 57 La Casa Grande Cigars

*Hand rolled the old-fashioned way*

Paul DiSilvio, founder and proprietor of La Casa Grande Cigars on Arthur Avenue, thought that rather than take a plane trip to the Dominican Republic to get hand-rolled stogies, why not bring the experience to the Bronx? Twenty years ago, he hired expert cigar rollers, imported his own tobacco leaves from Nicaragua and the Dominican Republic, and set up shop inside the Arthur Avenue Market. A master roller produces about 400 cigars per day, stacked in neat trays and placed in the walk-in humidor. "We started with a tiny booth that was no bigger than 10'x10' back then," DiSilvio says. "Arthur Avenue is known for handmade everything – sausage, cheeses, bread – so handmade cigars would go hand in hand."

The leaves come in big bales in a canvas-covered block, which are then separated, rolled, wrapped, and labeled. Each master roller makes a few dozen an hour. "It's taking a step into the old world of Cuba, Dominican, Tampa," DiSilvio says. "We are rediscovering the lost art of a culture – the gentlemen rolling the cigars here were in the business, each of them 30 or 40 years. They have experience because they were all supervisors and bosses at very well-known factories in the Dominican Republic. It's the Dream Team of cigar rolling." Five rollers keep busy, and you can watch them work.

There is a long list of celebrity cigar aficionados who DiSilvio has sold to, including Jennifer Aniston, Wyclef John, Remy Ma, Eric Stoltz, Joe Torre, and many hip-hop performers. Actor-playwright Chazz Palminteri is a regular, and La Casa Grande makes a "Bronx Tale" Cigar. "It's a tribute to the film and Arthur Avenue in the '50s and '60s. The cigar is a little piece of history you can bring home with you," DiSilvio says.

La Casa Grande offers cigar rolling classes by appointment. Arthur Avenue Market is filled with delicious Italian foods – you'll want to stay for lunch.

Address 2344 Arthur Avenue, Bronx, NY 10458, +1 (718)364-4657, www.lcgcigars.com, info@LCGcigars.com | **Getting there** Subway to Pelham Parkway (2, 5 train), then transfer to bus Bx12 to Fordham Road/Hoffman Street. Walk south on Arthur Avenue. | **Hours** Mon–Thu 9am–9pm, Fri & Sat 9am–9:30pm, Sun 9am–7pm | Tip Also inside the market is Mike's Deli, serving out-of-this-world Italian fare over the counter all day. Get the mozzarella, which the deli proclaims has two ingredients, "Made with love and Bronx water" (2344 Arthur Avenue, Bronx, NY 10458).

# 58 Liebman's Delicatessen

*One of the last of the great Jewish delis*

Since 1953, Liebman's has served an ocean's worth of matzo ball chicken soup. The changing neighborhood has a Spanish-speaking crew serving kosher fare to customers who come from across the borough to the Riverdale landmark. The potato knishes are old favorites made the same way since the Eisenhower administration.

Liebman's is one of the last Jewish delis left in the Bronx, a trend seen across New York. Before World War II, there were about 1,500 in the city, according to the *Times*. Today, only a handful are left in the Bronx, where there once were dozens. Jewish food can still be found in other restaurants, with other fare, but the stand-alone deli with photos of Woody Allen and Dustin Hoffman are disappearing. When Anthony Bourdain wanted a deli for his hit show *Parts Unknown*, this is where he went in the Bronx. He had a pastrami and corned beef, washed down with a Dr. Brown's cream soda.

Liebman's is a throwback to another era. Customers come in for booths in the back. The food preparation is still traditional. The meat slicer goes back and forth over the corned beef to begin the sandwich. Just enough is dropped onto a slice of brown bread with a swirl of mustard. A sliced tomato, dash of salt and pepper, then drop it on a plate. The final ingredients, two sliced dill pickles, complete the ritual. Liebman's has a "light" menu with healthy fare, but look at the old favorites. Try a Nova Platter with thinly sliced nova salmon, tomato, cucumber, green peppers, red onions, olives, capers, on a toasted bagel.

Their pastrami is made in-house, maybe the only deli in the borough that can claim that. The deli does a big business in to-go orders, to serve the customers who have left the Bronx and moved to New Jersey or Westchester, where there are even less Jewish delicatessens than in Riverdale. Kosher salami and liverwurst goes out the door.

Address 552 West 235th Street, Bronx, NY 10463, +1 (718)548-4534, www.liebmansdeli.com | Getting there Subway to 231st Street (1 train) | Hours Daily 10:30am–9:30pm | Tip Next door is the local wine shop, Riverdale Vintner. They have free tastings a few nights a week, with kosher wines served too (554 West 235th Street, Bronx, NY 10463, www.riverdalevintner.com).

# 59 Lindbergh Baby Kidnapper

*Sad story that helped G-men crack the case*

The sensational story of the kidnapping of Charles Lindbergh's baby boy on March 1, 1932 began in New Jersey, but nearly all of the major twists and turns took place in the Bronx. Twenty-month-old Charles Lindbergh, Jr. was taken from a second-story nursery by a kidnapper who scaled a homemade ladder at the famous aviator's home in Hopewell, New Jersey. Over the next month, the family received 13 ransom notes, and the kidnapper used Woodlawn Cemetery and St. Raymond's Cemetery as meeting points. Dr. John F. Condon, who acted as Lindbergh's middleman and delivered the $50,000 ransom in April 1932, lived at 2974 Decatur Avenue in Norwood. Condon used *The Bronx Home News* to post messages to the kidnapper. A month later, the murdered baby boy was found not far from the Lindbergh Estate back in New Jersey.

This case was the first to put the FBI into the spotlight. Agents tracked the ransom notes and gold $10 and $20 certificates, across New York in the coming months. Using old-fashioned shoe leather, agents fanned out to follow leads, which all led to the Bronx. When Bruno Richard Hauptmann, a carpenter and convicted criminal, spent one of the ransom notes at a gas station in Harlem in September 1934, the FBI cracked the case.

Hauptmann lived at 1279 East 222nd Street in Williamsbridge. The FBI found the ransom money and incriminating evidence on Hauptmann, and matched his handwriting with the notes. Portions of the ladder had been built from wood taken from the floorboards in this house's attic. Hauptmann was brought to the Bronx County Courthouse to be arraigned. The case was moved to New Jersey, where the trial was held. After a five-week trial, Hauptmann was found guilty and received the death penalty. His end came in the electric chair on April 3, 1936. More than 80 years later, both homes are still standing in nearly the same condition as they were in 1932.

**Address** 1279 East 222nd Street, Bronx, NY 10469 | **Getting there** Subway to Baychester Avenue (5 train), walk north one block on Thomas Brown Avenue, make a left on Boston Road. Walk five blocks to 222nd Street and make a right. | **Hours** Unrestricted from the outside only | **Tip** Try the microbrews at Gun Hill Brewing Company, which has a tasting room and live jazz. In the spirit of the Lindbergh case, try their Walk in the Woods, a cedar pale ale (3227 Laconia Avenue, Bronx, NY 10469, www.gunhillbrewing.com).

# 60__ The Lit. Bar
*The solitary borough bookstore*

For a few years, it was easier to find comic books and textbooks in the Bronx than the latest bestsellers in fiction. That all changed when a lone independent bookstore opened in Mott Haven in 2019, two years after the last chain store left the borough. The Lit. Bar, a bookstore and wine bar, came to the rescue for those that didn't want to go to Westchester County or Manhattan to browse the latest new books. The store opened to much fanfare and has been embraced by the South Bronx.

Proprietor Noëlle Santos was driven to open a bookstore for the 1.5 million residents who had to go without one. The store has rows of shelves on the sides so that events can take place in the middle. The Lit. Bar functions first as a bookstore. "We're general interest but we're located in the Bronx so most of our inventory reflects the community we live in, which is people of color," Santos says. "We have a little bit of everything. I definitely want to provide a platform for local authors, that is really important to me. Even when we did have a chain store in the Bronx it was limited with all the bureaucracy. As an independent bookstore, I'm the owner and the buyer, and I have a say with what goes on the shelves. So I'm really excited to provide local authors an opportunity."

The Lit. Bar opened with the idea to be more than a retailer of books. It was planned to be a gathering spot. "You can literally feel the culture spill out into the street, that's what's so special about the Bronx," Santos says. "When you come into the store you can feel that culture. From the design, inventory, food, it's a great place to meet people. Our neighborhood is gentrifying so it was important to me to have a space where the new residents and existing residents can have a discussion and become real neighbors. I couldn't think of a better way to bring people together than through literature and wine."

Address 131 Alexander Avenue, Bronx, NY 10454, www.thelitbar.com, thebronxreads@thelitbar.com | **Getting there** Subway to Third Avenue–138th Street (6 train) | **Hours** Daily 11am–10pm | **Tip** Book lover Saraciea Fennell founded the Bronx Book Festival, held annually in June at Fordham University. It's open to the public and draws local authors and hosts book talks (Fordham Plaza, Bronx, NY 10458, www.facebook.com/BronxBookFestival).

# 61 Loew's Paradise Theater
*Old Hollywood glamour takes the stage*

Days before the 1929 stock market crash devastated Wall Street, moviegoers in Fordham Heights were delighted by the sumptuous new movie palace that opened on the Grand Concourse. Loew's Paradise Theatre was a show palace for an audience of 4,000, so grand it was one of the five "Wonder Theaters" in the metro area. Each had a "Wonder Organ" and a massive screen. The design was over the top, with art influences from Egypt to Europe and cost $4 million (about $57 million today). The first film to unspool was *The Mysterious Dr. Fu-Manchu* starring Warner Oland. Its Italian Baroque-inspired façade, a style that was popular in the era, gave the theatergoer the feeling that they were entering another world. The man who designed the theater was credited with building more than 500 around the country, in a style that promoted illusion and wonderment.

Inside was a wonderland of fantasy. Architect John Eberson created "atmospheric" design, which many decades later theater visitors can still recall vividly from their youth. In place of a domed ceiling, he created a blue plaster "sky" with electric light bulbs to simulate stars. The walls were designed to mimic an Italian garden, so that moviegoers felt transported to a European opera house. Combined with plaster sculptures, painted interiors and golden detailing.

Like the rest of the movie business, the theater suffered from the popularity of TV, and filling 4,000 seats (and heating that big room) proved to be too great a challenge. It was chopped into two theaters and then transformed into four screens. Unlike the other Wonder Theaters, it continued to screen films until 1994, when it was boarded up. A multimillion-dollar restoration by entrepreneur Gerald Lieblich restored the theater to glory, and it reopened in 2005 as an event space and rental for churches. Graduation ceremonies, boxing matches, and music performances now take the stage where once movie stars were celebrated in glorious excess.

**Address** 2403 Grand Concourse, Bronx, NY 10468 | **Getting there** Subway to Fordham Road (B, D train) | **Tip** South of the theater is the Grand Concourse Historic District, created by the city in 2012. It begins on East 167th Street and extends to East 153rd Street, taking in 61 apartment houses, constructed 1917–1959. It's a must-see for fans of architectural history (www.hdc.org).

# 62 Longwood Historic District

*Survivors are recognized*

One of the smallest historic districts in the city is a tiny portion of the South Bronx carved out along East 156th Street. The Longwood Historic District was designated in 1980, and several more buildings were added later. The boundaries are south of Longwood Avenue between Beck Street and Prospect Avenue. Classic structures on Macy Place and Leggett Avenue are included, with a dip on Fox Street. Beautiful brownstones that were spared the widespread fires of the 1970s were saved; revitalization of the neighborhood through preservation has been a success. The National Register of Historic Places bestowed landmark status to the district in 1983.

Developer George B. Johnson purchased this piece of Morrisania in 1898. The area was relatively rural until the Interborough Rapid Transit Company (IRT) announced it was pushing subway lines into Morrisania. Johnson tapped architect Warren C. Dickerson to design the bulk of the houses, which are in the Renaissance and Romanesque Revival styles, notable for their polygonal or cone-shaped peak roofs, intricate brickwork, and columns around doors and windows. These two- and three-family homes were built between 1897 and 1900. Over on Hewitt Place are single-family homes designed by Charles C. Clark, who built many houses in the Bronx.

Start your exploration on Fox Street and Longwood Avenue. Weave north along Beck, Kelly, and Dawson Streets to spy fine examples of historic homes. 730 Kelly Street is a notable Dickerson design with its decorative elements. The homes are notable for bay windows, decorative trimming, and stained-glass windows. Many are set back from the street with stoops, adding to the spaciousness of the blocks. It's not just a fine tour, but a visible reminder of how a community saved their homes after the destructive era that stretched into the 1980s.

**Address** Fox Street and Longwood Avenue, Bronx, NY 10459, www.nypap.org/preservation-history/longwood-historic-district-community-association | **Getting there** Subway to Longwood Avenue (6 train), walk north on Longwood Avenue to Fox Street | **Hours** Unrestricted from the outside only | **Tip** For more than 30 years, sculptures cast of residents have been overlooking the neighborhood from a wall. *Life on Dawson Street* is the work of sculptors John Ahearn and Rigoberto Torres (911 Longwood Avenue, Bronx, NY 10459).

# 63 Making Batman, Batman

*Where co-creator Bill Finger dreamed up Gotham City*

Bill Finger was the co-creator and first writer of *Batman*, but illustrator Bob Kane took full credit for the character, forcing Finger to remain in the shadows. "Though Finger was a writer, the visual suggestions he made to Kane's first Bat-Man drawing were so key that, without them, the character might never have been published, and might not have lasted as long as he has," said Arlen Schumer, comics historian, illustrator, and author of *The Silver Age of Comic Book Art*.

Born in 1914, Finger lived in the Bronx in 1939 with his parents while writing *Batman*. He met with Kane in Poe Park. Kane pitched *Batman* to the publisher, claimed sole credit, and became rich. According to Schumer, not only did Finger define the "indelible iconography" of Batman – dark gray, cowl with slits for eyes, cape – he invented the entire Bat Universe.

"The problem was," Schumer continues, "Kane got the credit from DC Comics for everything Finger created in that first Batman issue of *Detective Comics* (#27), and all the issues to come, like the names Bruce Wayne, Dick Grayson, and Gotham City, and all the Bat-accoutrements, like the Batmobile and the Batcave. When it came to creating the other main characters – Robin and Alfred, and Batman's major villains, The Joker, The Penguin, Catwoman – Kane and Finger would have discussions first, soon joined by Bob's first *Batman* ghost artist, Jerry Robinson. They'd all contribute something… but Kane got all the credit because his was the only name was on the strip!"

Finger died a penniless alcoholic at 59, "alone and unmourned," Schumer says. Kane came clean in his 1989 autobiography. For decades fans demanded that Finger be recognized. In 2015, the credit line "Batman created by Bob Kane with Bill Finger" appeared in DC Comics. The Bronx celebrated the "Bill Finger Way" street naming on East 192nd Street and Grand Concourse two years later.

Address 2754 Grand Concourse, Bronx, NY 10458 | **Getting there** Subway to Kingsbridge Road (B, D train) | **Hours** Unrestricted | **Tip** To find out what Batman is doing today, visit nearby Fordham Comics. In addition to current issues, the store is a hub for Magic: The Gathering fans. The shop also hosts Friday game nights (390 East Fordham Road, Bronx, NY 10458).

# 64 Marble Hill ZIP Code

*Are we in the Bronx?*

Geography nerds all know that the Bronx is the only one of the five boroughs of New York City attached to the mainland United States. But the true local geography lover has knowledge of Marble Hill. This neighborhood is included on maps as being a sliver of Manhattan. Technically part of the Bronx (walk across the street), it was formed when Spuyten Duyvil Creek was filled with landfill in 1895. This turned the island neighborhood of Marble Hill – strategically important during the Revolutionary War – into a part of the Bronx, while remaining legally tied to Manhattan in name.

Marble Hill residents are called for jury duty in Manhattan and cast ballots for Manhattan city council members and other elected office holders. However, their children are in Bronx school districts and Bronx precincts and fire companies protect them. They live in the 10034 ZIP code. "104" prefix is for Bronx addresses, Manhattan uses "100." For some, it's been a long-simmering feeling of wonderment. In a 1939 publicity stunt, Bronx borough president James Lyons planted a flag on the banks of Manhattan and claimed it "Bronx Sudetenland" (Hitler had recently annexed Czechoslovakia). Today, local history fans led by Isaac Moore of the Great and Glorious Grand Army of the Bronx, "with the sole mission of enforcing Bronx awesomeness on the mainland," reenact the flag-planting annually.

Walking across the Broadway Bridge, to say "it looks and feels like the Bronx" isn't enough. The boundaries follow where the river once flowed. The streets north of the river were given Dutch names and have fine single-family homes. The U-shaped street that was the location of the waterway is named Van Corlear Place for colonist Anthony Van Corlaer, and Jacobus Place, for Jacobus Dyckman, who sponsored the first local bridge. Adrian Avenue honors Adriaen van der Donck, a Dutch settler and developer.

Address Intersection of West 225th Street and Broadway, Bronx, NY 10034 | Getting there Subway to Marble Hill (1 train) | Hours Unrestricted | Tip From the platform of the Marble Hill and 225th Street subway station is a scenic view of the water, the borough of Manhattan, and Marble Hill (West 225th Street and Broadway, New York, NY 10463).

# 65  Mel's Locksmith
*The small business with a lock on tradition*

Ray Herskovitz has been making keys for more than 50 years from a Mount Eden location that is so tiny it gives new meaning to "small business." In Mel's Locksmith – where three customers can barely squeeze inside – the size of the shop doesn't matter to Ray. "How much room do you need? You're only coming in to get a key."

He inherited the business from his late father, who passed away at 102. Except for his Army service, Ray has been a neighborhood fixture for more than 70 years.

"I made my first key when I was probably five," Ray recalls. "As a kid, I worked weekends here with my father." The shop had humble beginnings. "During the Depression everyone lost their job," Ray said. "A relation gave my uncle Jerome a key machine to keep him occupied. He and my father Mel were very close. They had a key wagon from 1932 to 1937."

The pushcart was such a success they decided to open a brick-and-mortar store to get out of the weather. The shop measured just 26 inches by 42 inches – a reporter tabbed it the "Smallest Shop in the Entire United States." They moved to a slightly larger space, Mel's Lock & Key Service. The store has always been on East 170th Street and has never gotten much larger than about 125 square feet.

Ray has cut tens of thousands of keys over the decades; some went into the pockets of boldface names. Comedian Jackie Gleason feared robberies, so Ray changed the locks on his safes constantly. Actress Lucille Ball, like many stars long ago, carried personal door cylinders when travelling. Ray went to fancy hotels to put in new locks to keep hotel staff (and others) out.

He looks at working as a hobby. "It's a habit, after you've been doing it for 52 years," Ray says. "The mental stimulation is good for my mind. I recalibrate the cutters when they need it. At my age I'll be more aware of Alzheimer's."

Address 4 East 170th Street, Bronx, NY 10452, +1 (718)538-3972 | Getting there Subway to 170th Street (4 train) | Hours Mon, Tue & Thu–Sat 10am–3pm | Tip Walk around the corner for colorful and intriguing street art that's been there for over 20 years (Townsend Avenue between 170th and 171st Streets, Bronx, NY 10452).

# 66 Mosholu Parkway

*Beautifying a roadway with greenery*

The Algonquin Indian word "mosholu" means "smooth stones" and was the original name for Tibbett's Creek running in Van Cortlandt Park. Mosholu Parkway connects Van Cortlandt Park to Bronx Park and is not only a major traffic artery, but also a neighborhood recreation area in Norwood. The wide, grassy parkway is lined with red maple and oak trees, part of the late 19th-century plan for building parks in the city. Only 600 feet wide at parts, it stretches 1.4 miles. Mosholu Parkway was designed so residents could ride their carriages and bicycles from one park to another; Bronx Park contains both the New York Botanical Garden and the Zoo. The "parkway" was a new concept driven by pioneering park landscape architect Frederick Law Olmsted.

The variety of natural beauty in the park is high. Dogwood, forsythia, lilac, and magnolia bloom in spring. Oak trees surround the two large playgrounds in the park. All of the trees and landscaping is planned, dispelling the legend that the entire park was once a forest dating to the Colonial era. Bike paths attract kids learning to ride and cyclists. Mosholu Parkway is part of the TrailLink Rails-to-Trails Conservancy cycling route for the Mosholu-Pelham Greenway, a 10.3-mile ride (www.traillink.com). The parkway does, of course, extend north. In the 1930s, master builder Robert Moses pushed the roadway directly across the center of Van Cortlandt Park to link to his Henry Hudson Parkway. The park lost precious acres, including important marshlands, to the highways.

The baseball field at Webster Avenue between East 201st Street and Mosholu Parkway is named for Hall of Fame member Frankie Frisch. He ran track for Fordham Prep and Fordham University, where he picked up his nickname, the Fordham Flash. In the summer, Frisch Field is the location for outdoor movies provided by NYC Department of Parks and Recreation.

Address Mosholu Parkway South and Webster Avenue, Bronx, NY 10458 | Getting there
Subway to Belford Park Boulevard (4, D train) | Hours Unrestricted | Tip The park is home to
the lovely Harvest Home North Central Bronx Farmers Market on Mosholu Parkway North
and Jerome Avenue on Wednesdays, from June to November (www.harvesthomecfm.org).

# 67 Mott Haven Historic District

*Unique buildings are a window to the past*

For more than a century, Mott Haven supplied the iron that was used in construction, from decorative fences to reinforced concrete. When Jordan L. Mott established his iron empire here in 1828, it transformed this corner of Morrisania from pastoral to industrial (see ch. 93). It also brought tens of thousands of residents. Most new homes were commonplace designs, but many were wonderful and worth preserving within the Mott Haven Historic District, situated along Alexander Avenue, bounded by East 137th Street to the south, and East 141st Street to the north.

The district was the first in the borough to be designated historic in 1969, not long after Brooklyn Heights. As you wander the neighborhood, it can be hard to imagine the area was once home to a booming industrial site that employed thousands. Some of the better-paid workers took homes here of yellow and dark brick, with stained-glass windows and elaborate interiors with fireplaces and carved wood entrances. This residential stretch of Alexander Avenue was nicknamed "The Irish Fifth Avenue," "Doctor's Row," and "Politician's Row," and is today home to a vibrant community. Two notable buildings are the Mott Haven Branch of the New York Public Library (1905) (see ch. 1) and St. Jerome's Roman Catholic Church (1898).

Two more areas were designated by the Landmarks Preservation Commission in 1994. The Mott Haven East Historic District is located on East 139th and East 140th Street between Brook and Willis Avenues. The Bertine Block Historic District, named for the yellow brick brownstones designed by Edward Bertine between 1891 and 1895, is located on East 136th Street, also between Brook and Willis Avenues. Thanks to history-minded residents and preservation, these unique streets are preserved.

Address Alexander Avenue and East 137th Street, Bronx, NY 10454, www.mcny.org/story/mott-haven-historic-district | Getting there Subway to Third Avenue–East 137th Street (6 train) | Tip South Bronx Historical Tours offers a walk through the neighborhood with detailed stories about the area. The tours are run by Alexandra Maruri, Bronx native and member of the Guides Association of NYC (www.bronxhistoricaltours.com).

# 68 Mott Iron Works Sign

*Ghostly reminder of a factory town*

In Mott Haven on the side of 2403 Third Avenue is a remnant of the neighborhood's industrial past. From the Third Avenue Bridge, look for *J. L. Mott Iron Works* signage. It's in the brick façade, made of brick letters about 10-feet high. The sign can be viewed from the pedestrian bridge and the street.

In 1841, the southwestern corner of the borough was sold to Jordan Lawrence Mott, an entrepreneur and inventor of iron stoves. Mott made two innovations to iron kitchen cooking stoves, which were relatively new. First, they were aesthetically handsome with smooth castings and decoratively designed. Second, they burned anthracite, not wood. With so many new products, his Manhattan-based business grew quickly (Mott Street is named for him), and he needed more space to continue to innovate and expand his manufacturing capacity. He chose the location on the Harlem River and built up a small factory town. Not modest, he named it Mott Haven. Immigrants from Ireland were coming to New York in droves, and Mott hired many of them to work in all capacities in his factory.

Around the time of the Civil War, the area was booming for Mott and his family. Factories made of wood caught fire and burned down, replaced by stout brick structures. The stoves made the family wealthy, and they expanded production. Mott Iron Works also created bathtubs, boilers, coal chutes, sinks, and decorative wrought iron for gardens and fencing. The work was incredibly detailed and artistic. Illustrated trade catalogs created by Mott craftsmen are today held by the Smithsonian National Museum of American History. Vintage iron pieces made here by Mott artisans are valued antique collectibles.

Eventually the business outgrew even Mott Haven and the plant was moved to Trenton, New Jersey. This eye-catching sign is the last remnant in the area where the business once flourished.

**Address** 2403 Third Avenue, Bronx, NY 10451 | **Getting there** Subway to 138th Street–Third Avenue (6 train) | **Hours** Unrestricted | **Tip** Walk 10 minutes to East 136th Street between Willis and Brook Avenues, and you'll be in the middle of the Bertine Block Historic District. These beautiful homes take their name from developer Edward D. Bertine, who built the first Queen Anne-style residences in the 1870s. The eye-catching brickwork and stained-glass windows are a time trip back to old Mott Haven (www.mhhda.org).

# 69 Mottley Kitchen
*Coffee and community in a cozy space*

Chef Kat Creech was looking to open a catering business in the South Bronx in 2017. But when she found this location, she knew it would also make a perfect café and bakery. And Mottley Kitchen was born. Its stunning, open-air space and steel and brick architecture wins raves from the neighborhood, but it's the fresh-baked pastries, breakfast, and chocolate bars that keep everyone coming back.

"I'm most proud this is all about community and sharing space," Creech said. "People come in and spend time together." On weekends, families with kids come in for the Saturday morning book read-alongs with authors. There's been yoga and arts and crafts. The spot has become a neighborhood gathering place with rotating artist exhibitions; every two months a different Bronx creator is displayed on the walls.

And people are drawn to Mottley Kitchen for the food. Creech says the popular lunch option is a Green Goddess Bowl: arugula, daily grain, feta cheese, and avocado, topped with crunchy chickpeas, pistachios, parsley, and an herb buttermilk dressing. It's a vegetarian stop for breakfast, and the cup of overnight oats is a big seller: rolled, gluten-free oats, house turmeric spice blend, blackberries, macadamia nut milk, and nut butter, sweetened with agave. While the owners bake in-house from scratch, they partner with others for supplies. They get their beans locally from Uptown Roasters and their meat and poultry from Brooklyn.

Kat and husband David are Bronx residents who are also hiring staff from the neighborhood. The catering business shares the kitchen, and it stays busy with clients around the city eager to support a business with locally grown ingredients and fresh-baked pastries. The Kitchen is hopping, and the dining room is popular for baby showers and photo shoots. Future plans include creating additional space on the roof.

Address 402 East 140th Street, Bronx, NY 10454, +1 (929)308-2099, www.mottleykitchen.com, kat@mottleykitchen.com | Getting there Subway to Brook Avenue (6 train) | Hours Tue–Fri 7:30am–4pm, Sat 8am–5pm | Tip The pop-up books for sale in the café come from Boogie Down Books. Proprietor Rebekah Shoaf programs young adult and children's authors to come in, chooses new books, and delivers books around the borough for sales and signings. Kids and teens are their specialty (www.boogiedownbooks.com).

# 70 Museum of the Arts

*Stroll among the canvases to celebrate the visual*

One of the best places in New York to experience contemporary visual art and see emerging artists and performers is the Bronx Museum of the Arts. It launched 45 years ago as a scrappy arts spot inside the unused rotunda of the Bronx County Courthouse. Today, it occupies a soaring 16,000-square-foot art space that has won design awards. Major pieces by artists of historical significance line its galleries. The permanent collection includes Vito Acconci, Alvin Baltrop, Elizabeth Catlett, Juan Downey, Raphael Montañez Ortiz, and Martin Wong.

Walking into this museum isn't like one in Manhattan because the first thing that's noticeable in the vestibule in giant letters is *FREE ADMISSION*. The museum has a laid-back feel, more like a gallery than a major cultural institution. It doesn't offer maps or audio guides like bigger institutions, what they offer is soaring, quiet space, and lots of it. The spaces are expansive and well lit, easy to access, and move around. There are two main large galleries with smaller ones attached.

The museum owns more than 2,000 contemporary artworks in all media, and its mission is to reflect the diversity of the Bronx and represent the borough's history. When the collection was initiated in 1986, it began collecting works on paper by artists of African, Asian, and Latin American ancestry. Today, it features artists from around the world who have a direct connection to the Bronx. Among these artists are Romare Bearden (US), Xu Bing (China), Tania Bruguera (Cuba), Seydou Keita (Mali), Dinh Q. Le (Vietnam), Nikki S. Lee (Korea), Ana Mendieta (Cuba), Helio Oiticica (Brazil), Pepon Osorio (Puerto Rico), Liliana Porter (Argentina), Juan Sanchez (US), and Kara Walker (US).

The museum has a café and event space with ongoing public programming, from talks to live music. On Friday nights it hosts a happy hour from 5 to 8pm.

Address 1040 Grand Concourse, Bronx, NY 10456, www.bronxmuseum.org | Getting there Subway to 167th Street (B, D train) | Hours Sat, Sun, Wed & Thu 11am–6pm, Fri 11am–8pm | Tip Art Deco style abounds among Grand Concourse apartment buildings. One of the most famous American architects, Emery Roth, created a gem on the southeast corner of 161st Street in 1937. Look inside to see the lobby's compass pattern on the floor – but remember this is private property (888 Grand Concourse, Bronx, NY 10451).

# 71_Music Heritage Center

*Teaching the next generation of music creators*

In the Crotona East section is an institution that holds free live music shows, film screenings, poetry readings, and talks about the music that was born and popularized in the Bronx. The Bronx Music Heritage Center (BMHC) tells the story of the borough and its ties to mambo, salsa, hip-hop, and rap. There are frequent exhibitions that explore African-American and Afro-Latino culture. The organization presents live cultural performances and provides low-cost music education for the South Bronx.

The BMHC is part of Intervale Green, a building of affordable housing supported by the Women's Housing and Economic Development Corporation. The space is simply designed with a concrete floor and exposed ceiling pipes and lighting, but the room itself is full of creative energy. It has a piano, drums, and instruments lined up. The wall art is by TATS Cru. BMHC draws from the area for teachers of music and performance, and the students then give their own public performance.

Award-winning folklorist Elena Martinez and Grammy-nominated Bronx musician Bobby Sanabria curate the events. For 10 years, programs have been offered on a wide range of topics. Martinez runs the "Bronx Rising!" film, music, and spoken word series monthly, showcasing rising stars and veteran performers from the Bronx. There are also free and low-cost concerts in the intimate space. Among the performers have been bassist Andy Gonzalez and hip-hop pioneer DJ Kool Herc (see ch. 25).

An ongoing series of exhibits and installations is a longtime feature of the BMHC, including street photography, paintings, illustrations, and digital art as some of the rotating shows. The spot is also the place for classes and workshops for children and adults. Salsa classes are among the most popular offerings. The BMHC radiates creativity and is one of the best places in the borough to spot rising music stars.

**Address** 1303 Louis Niñé Boulevard, Bronx, NY 10459, +1 (347)708-7591, www.thisisbronxmusic.org, emartinez@whedco.org | **Getting there** Subway to Freeman Street (2, 5 train) | **Hours** See website for classes and events | **Tip** If boxing is the workout you need, nearby El Maestro Boxing Gym, next to El Maestro Community Center, may be the place for you (1300 Southern Boulevard, Bronx, NY 10459).

# 72__New York Pole Dancing
*Tricks for fun, fitness, and endurance to the max*

Wendy Traskos slips on eight-inch high-heel pumps and climbs a pole eleven feet high in her Mott Haven studio. As she gracefully kicks her long legs out, she spins around the pole, making it obvious that she loves what she does for a living. Traskos is the founder and lead instructor of New York Pole Dancing, the oldest pole studio in the city. She opened her studio almost 15 years ago and moved it from Hell's Kitchen to the South Bronx for more space, which now accommodates a class of 16 students on eight poles that reach 10.5' and 11.5'.

"I danced years ago in clubs," Traskos said. "I learned five tricks and did them over and over again. It was such a great workout. When I stopped dancing and started personal training, my friend said they were starting to do pole dancing out in California for fitness, and she wanted me to be the first one to open a studio in New York. I started with about 500 square feet of space and expanded."

Traskos grew the business by appealing to a mix of bachelorette parties and fitness clients. It's generally not strippers who come to New York Pole. "We get a lot of accountants, doctors, nurses, and teachers," Traskos said. "They are in careers that don't allow them to express themselves or to have fun because they're in 'serious' jobs."

"Pole dancing is so great for anybody," she said. "Mainly it's women, but we get some men in here. It's resistance training, flexibility training, and endurance training. Overall it brings everything together, plus you get to express yourself. It's a win-win for people who are in industries that don't let them explore their own creativity."

Traskos says the students mostly fall in the 25–35 age range, but she sees women in their 40s, 50s, and even 60s. "For me it's the expression and the hard work that goes into it. Because you get to express yourself, you feel good. You leave the class feeling invigorated."

Address 503 East 137th Street, 3rd Floor, Bronx, NY 10454, +1 (718)292-2904, www.nypoledancing.com, nypdstaff@gmail.com | Getting there Subway to Brook Avenue (6 train) | Hours Check website for class schedule | Tip Is the most famous male dancer from the Bronx named Al Pacino? The actor's sole Oscar win was for *Scent of a Woman*, in which he danced the tango. His single mother raised him in her parent's home in Crotona Park East (1685 Bryant Avenue, Bronx, NY 10460).

# 73 __ Night Market
*Eat your way around the world – on Fordham Road*

The diversity of the borough is on display for all to see and experience at the monthly Bronx Night Market, which was launched in 2018 on Fordham Plaza. The Saturday night festival brings together artists, brewers, cooks, makers, and musicians for a multisensory experience. Big crowds are drawn to the free open-air event by the delicious and cheap eats (about $3–$7) and live music. The market was a hit out of the gate, drawing 10,000 people each night.

Sample tasty bites from Albania to Spain to Mexico and make your own "to eat list" as you wander around. Many of the food vendors have restaurants and bring their best fare at the night market. There is a beer and wine garden with craft beverages flowing. The Bronx Brewery (see ch. 15) and Bronx Beer Hall are vendors with their new products on tap; Milea vineyards serve wine from Staatsburg.

The night market launched as collaboration with three groups that wanted to bring people together. The quarterly magazine *Edible Bronx* (www.ediblebronx.ediblecommunities.com) covers borough chefs, food news, gardens, and restaurants. BLOX (www.blox.nyc) is a Bronx-based creative agency that has developed the branding for many young entrepreneurs, startups, and local brands. The Fordham Road Business Improvement District serves the community.

The Bronx Night Market has more than 35 food vendors, handcrafted items, art merchants, and live entertainment. A requirement for being a vendor is that they are local to the Bronx, and the organizers think they managed "99 percent" compliance with the festival. In addition to being Bronx-based, the vendors were curated to build and showcase a global experience. So you will not find 25 taco stands, but rather a much more wide-ranging food experience. Among the vendors are Born Juice, Higher Dining, Il Forno Bakery, In Patella, La Cantina, Lotsa Latkes, and Next Stop Vegan.

Address 1 Fordham Plaza, Bronx, NY 10455, www.thebronxnightmarket.com | Getting there Subway to Fordham Road (B, D train), walk 0.5 miles west, or Metro-North to Fordham | Hours Last Saturday of the month 4–11pm; check website for schedule | Tip Fordham Road is the main shopping avenue in the borough. You'll find clothes, jewelry, shoes, and more. It's also lined with restaurants and discount stores on this one-mile stretch between Webster Avenue and Southern Boulevard (Fordham Road, Bronx, NY 10458).

# 74_ NY Marathon Cheer Zone

*With the end in sight, the runners need you here*

The New York Marathon is the biggest spectator sport in the city, drawing 2.5 million to cheer on the runners. After running the first segment in Manhattan, the 50,000+ runners enter the Bronx. This is where you will find one of the best vantage points of the course. This is Mile 20. Pick a spot at 138th Street and Alexander Avenue and help the runners break through "the wall" as they face the final miles. Look for the baroque Church of St. Jerome as a landmark. This is the hub of the South Bronx and a good place to spend the day showing support for the runners as they pass.

Runner Nicole Trotman has completed the marathon three times and remembers well the pain and exhilaration of crossing the Willis Avenue Bridge and the surge of energy as she entered Mott Haven. "The race goes over the bridge, and then you're in the South Bronx," the Fordham University grad recalls. "You're starting to realize that you're doing a marathon at that point. That's when it starts to hit you. That's when you start to get tired, that's when all the training you've done comes into play. The Bronx, for me, is the hardest because at that point I'm tired. I know I'm almost there at the finish line, but it's still a struggle."

The Bronx mile part of the route is among the most spirited – and crucial – as runners test their endurance. Bells, drums, salsa music, and cheers come from the streets. "It's exciting because you know that you're almost at the finish line. A lot of the urban running crews in the city have a cheer zone at Mile 21. So your objective is to get to the Bronx, run through it, and once you cross over the Madison Avenue Bridge you know you're going to be greeted by your run family. Mentally, you're saying, 'I want to get there. I want to see my family.' I really enjoyed it, the crowd was great! They play music and it's very lively. It stops you from obsessing about getting to the finish line."

Address East 138th Street and Alexander Avenue, Bronx, NY 10454, www.nyrr.org | Getting there Subway to 138th Street (4, 6 train) | Hours Annually first Sunday in November; see website for training runs and community events | Tip Among the area urban running crews taking to the streets are the Boogie Down Bronx Runners (www.facebook.com/boogiedownbronxrunners) who hold a weekly 5K at 7pm at 785 Pelham Parkway. The Bronx Nomads (www.instagram.com/bronxnomads) run the Williamsbridge Oval twice weekly.

# 75 Old Veterans Cemetery

*A forlorn spot in West Farms*

It is easy to miss the sad little cemetery unless you know it is there. Old West Farms Soldiers' Cemetery, at 180th Street and Bryant Avenue, dates to the early 19th century. Over the decades, more than 40 veterans were interred here who served in every conflict from the War of 1812 to World War I. The last soldier buried was Private Valeriano J. Tolosa, a native of the Philippines, in 1929. In 1967, the cemetery was among the first places in the borough to be granted historic status by the Landmarks Preservation Commission.

The tiny cemetery – just 0.64 acres – was established by the Beck Memorial Presbyterian Church in 1814 and has more than 100 graves. Long ago, there was a statue of a Union soldier, vintage field guns mounted on carriages, and white picket fences. The statue went missing, the cannons vanished, and the fence is now ornate back iron. The cemetery became so neglected the city took it over. The American Legion successfully lobbied for its rescue, and today the City Department of Parks maintains it.

In the past, when a preservation society tended the cemetery, it got more attention. For Memorial Day 1916, a steamboat brought six coffins from Hart Island with the remains of Civil War veterans removed from a soldiers' plot. A crowd of Bronxites observed a solemn New York National Guard ceremony that led a procession from a dock on East 132nd Street to the cemetery. Brought for reburial were Pvt. Henry Grub, 103rd New York; Pvt. Edward McGrath, 163rd New York; Lt. Robert McLaughlin, 25th New York; Pvt. Conrad Neycomer, 9th New Jersey; Pvt. John T. Smith, 32nd Illinois; and August Weicking, who served in the Army as a private and the Navy on the frigate USS *Merrimac* and sidewheeler USS *Winooski*.

Today, neighbors clean up the park and hold community veterans memorial ceremonies. The gates are unlocked twice a year for visitors.

Address 180th Street and Bryant Avenue, Bronx, NY 10460 | Getting there Subway to 180th Street (2, 5 train) | Hours Viewable from outside the gate; open Memorial Day & Veterans Day | Tip One of the saddest places in Bronx history is the Happy Land Memorial. In 1990, a madman set the Happy Land social club ablaze, killing 87, the majority of whom were Honduran immigrants. The location was west of this stone monument (1955 Southern Boulevard, Bronx, NY 10460, www.nycgovparks.org/parks/crotona-parkway-malls/monuments/1772).

# 76 Opera House Hotel

*From Broadway stars to a good night's sleep*

The Bronx has dozens of abandoned theaters that today have been given a second life as churches, furniture stores, gyms, and pharmacies. Where once audiences came to be entertained, now they shop for potato chips or refrigerators. However, the Bronx Opera House, one of the grandest of the pre-World War I-era playhouses, lives on as boutique hotel, maintaining some of the grandeur of its past life. The Opera House was once a stage on the "subway circuit" that brought big stars from Broadway. The Barrymores, Eddie Cantor, George M. Cohan, and the Marx Brothers all played here.

"The subway circuit was a way for actors to be on the road and at home in New York at the same time," says author Noah Diamond. "Shows that were either on their way from Broadway to the road, or less frequently shows that were from the road and going to Broadway. It was this middle ground because it was New York – about six theaters – that you could reach using the New York City subway. And the subway itself was only 10 years old, so this whole thing was dazzlingly modern. Tickets were cheaper, but the people who worked on the shows got paid the same. It was standard practice at the time that a show would be on the road before and after Broadway. If it did well on the road in its initial run, they would bring it into New York."

Designed by George Kiester, the same architect as the Apollo Theater in Harlem, the playhouse had close to 2,000 seats and two balconies. Vaudeville saw the end of live entertainment in the 1930s, and the Opera House became a movie theater after World War II. For 30 years, it was a Latin music ballroom, until it was rented to a church. In 2007, hotelier Jay Bomb rescued the historic building, razed the condemned auditorium, and built an upscale hotel. It reopened in 2013 with 60 suites and rooms. Step into the lobby and imagine bumping into Groucho or Harpo.

Address 436 East 149th Street, Bronx, NY 10455, +1 (718)407-2800, www.operahousehotel.com | Getting there Subway to 149th Street – Third Avenue (2, 5 train) | Hours Unrestricted from the outside | Tip Legendary comic strip artist Ernie Bushmiller (1905 – 1982) is from this neighborhood. He was born here and said local comedy shows influenced him. Bushmiller created one of the most influential strips of all time, Nancy (658 East 161st Street, Bronx, NY 10456).

# 77___Origin of the Hip-Hop DJ
## *The education of Grandmaster Flash*

Hip-hop culture was born in the Bronx out of four crucial elements: b-boying (break dancing), DJing, graffiti, and rapping (MCing). All intermingled. The three core DJs to emerge from this era – Afrika Bambaataa of Soundview, DJ Kool Herc (see ch. 25) in the West Bronx, and Grandmaster Flash in the South Bronx – are generally credited as the pioneers. Part of the lore of the career of Grandmaster Flash was that he was an electronics wizard and genius at wiring and engineering the earliest equipment to launch the sound of this new art form. This is where he started, Samuel Gompers Industrial High School.

Born Joseph Saddler in Barbados, his childhood was bleak as he moved through foster homes as a young boy. In high school, his inquisitive mind led him to learn basic electronics and how to wire audio equipment. This was right when the culture of street parties and performances in community centers was rising. He built his own equipment and worked with many, many people as the nascent industry took off in the mid-1970s.

Flash and his crew included the Livingston Brothers (the L Brothers) of DJ Mean Gene, Cordeo, and Theodore (Grand Wizzard Theodore) (see ch. 49). "It was amazing man, being a part of a culture," Theodore said. "This was our way of dealing with all of the drugs, single parent homes, going to school and not learning anything, and all the abandoned buildings and fires in the Bronx. Basically what we did to amuse ourselves, we b-boyed, we did graffiti, we MC'd, we DJ'd – that's how hip-hop was formed. Something to get our minds off all of the everyday ups and downs we were going through in the inner city."

In 2007, Grandmaster Flash and the Furious Five were the first hip-hop performers inducted into the Rock & Roll Hall of Fame. Flash continues to DJ today. His alma mater closed in 2015 and the building is now home to three schools.

Address 455 Southern Boulevard, Bronx, NY 10455 | Getting there Subway to East 143rd Street–St. Mary's Street (6 train) | Hours Unrestricted from the outside only | Tip The Netflix series *The Get Down* was filmed in the neighborhood, including nearby St. Mary's Park. Grandmaster Flash served as associate producer of the series about the early days of hip-hop (450 St Ann's Avenue, Bronx, NY 10455, www.nycgovparks.org/parks/st-marys-park).

# 78_ Our Lady of Lourdes Grotto

*Where the holy water flows*

The faithful do not need to travel to France to fill up their bottles with holy water at Our Lady of Lourdes. Just go to St. Lucy's Roman Catholic Church in Allerton. You can fill up at the church's own outdoor grotto. It was dedicated in 1939, and like its famous counterpart in Lourdes, it draws the faithful in big numbers.

The water that flows from the grotto is New York City tap water blessed annually by the church. Under the watchful gaze of Mary, a small crowd lines up with containers of all sizes to fill up. On warm days, some pour the water over their heads; others drink it out of their hands and splash it on children's faces. Dabbing it on the eyes is a tradition, as St. Lucy, the parish namesake, is the patron saint of the blind and those with vision trouble. At the grotto, look up and see the rosary beads hanging nearby. At your feet is a metal grate to catch the overflowing water. Some devotees drop loose change and small bills into it. At the outdoor altar, more than 250 candles are placed in long rows.

While holy water bottles are a common sight for home use, don't be surprised to spot gallon milk jugs and other containers slowly being filled up. That's because some are taking the holy water home to drink or bathe with. Others use it to wash cars to ward off collisions.

In the yard next to the church and grotto are three rows of outdoor pews for quiet prayer and reflection. The area is calm and peaceful; it's one of the few spots where nobody is on their phones.

A trip to St. Lucy's has to include visiting the 1928 church. Mass is offered daily in English and Spanish, and Albanian and Italian on weekends. Do not miss the Hall of Saints. Inside are more than 25 carved sculptures of saints, from the famous to the lesser known. Through a doorway is a small church shop selling candles, rosary beads, statues of every size, and medals.

Address 833 Mace Avenue, Bronx, NY 10467, +1 (718)882-0710, www.stlucybronx.org, stlucybronx@gmail.com | Getting there Subway to Allerton Avenue (2, 5 train) | Hours Daily 9am–5pm weather permitting | Tip For all two-wheel needs, the locals go to the Bikelery. These pros sell and service all models from Anza, to Cannondale, and Schwinn. The wide range of bikes can handle the notoriously poor pavements of the neighborhood. Look for the lazy shop cat snoozing on the counter (2557 Boston Road, Bronx, NY 10467, www.thebikelery.com).

# 79___Our Lady of Mount Carmel

*Immigrants decorated a church with passion*

The interior of the century-old Our Lady of Mount Carmel rivals that of St. Patrick's Cathedral on Fifth Avenue. If you happen to be noshing along Arthur Avenue, duck into this Old World church. What puts the neighborhood church on any must-visit list is the attention the parish has devoted to art and sculpture. Immigrant artists created the ceiling murals after World War I. The dozens of carved sculptures are meticulously maintained for saints tied to the neighborhood.

Italian immigrants that moved to Belmont to build the subways also built the parish. They asked the diocese to build a church for an Italian-speaking priest. In this era, more than 200,000 Italians lived in the Bronx. A storefront mission opened in 1906, the parish continued to grow, and Our Lady of Mount Carmel was dedicated in 1917. Over the ensuing years, it became one of the largest Italian churches in the country with 40,000 parishioners and nine priests.

The first notable features upon entering – if you can take your eyes off the magnificent ceiling artwork – are the four beautiful carved stone fonts at the back of the church. These are just some of the many fine religious artworks throughout the interior.

Today, mass is offered in English, Italian, and Spanish and a Latin American population has filled the church. If you can be in attendance to watch a *Quinceañera* – a girl's 15th birthday party – it's like witnessing a mini-wedding without a groom. All of the major holidays, the church is heavily decorated. On the right side of the church, look at the shrine to the three key saints that have strong ties to the Hispanic members of the parish. Each feast day is celebrated here grandly. They are Our Lady of Guadalupe, Patron Saint of the Americas and Mexico; Our Lady of Divine Providence, principal patroness of Puerto Rico; and Our Lady of Altagracia, Protector and Queen of the Dominicans.

**Address** 627 East 187th Street, Bronx, NY 10458, +1 (718)295-3770, www.ourladymtcarmelbx.org | **Getting there** Bus Bx17 to Crotona Avenue/East 187th Street | **Hours** See website for schedule | **Tip** Across the street is a pastry shop that's been beloved since 1912. Egidio Pastry has been baking cakes to traditional Italian recipes for more than a century. Their espresso is renowned throughout the neighborhood (622 East 187th Street, Bronx, NY 10458, www.facebook.com/Egidiospastries).

# 80_Pelham Bay Park

*Tidal pools of the biggest park of all*

Orchard Beach is New York's Riviera with more than one mile of white, crescent-shaped sand and gently lapping waves from Pelham Bay. Is this really New York? With 13 miles of saltwater shoreline, Pelham Bay Park is New York City's largest park, three times bigger than Central Park. Orchard Beach has swimming, promenade, and paths that lead to tidal pools and wetlands. A walk in Pelham Bay Park is not much different today than when the Siwanoy tribe sold the land to Englishman Thomas Pell in 1654, except for the planes from nearby La Guardia Airport.

In the 1880s, the city bought the land to create the 2,763-acre park. The beach – a fraction of the size it is today – was not widely used until master builder Robert Moses came along in the 1930s. Using Depression-era funding, he transformed the park with an army of workers to give more Bronxites access. The size of the park and combination of old growth forest, open water, rare coastal tall grass meadows, rocky shore, salt marsh, scrubland, and young forest make it an incredibly diverse biosphere to enjoy.

Off the beach, look for Twin Islands Preserve Trail; it leads to one of the last remaining salt marshes in the region. In Twin Islands' tidal pool at low tide is easy to spot clams, small fish, and oysters. For kids in the summer, Urban Park Rangers lead free exploration trips to view the tidal pools. A good selfie spot is on the northeastern edge of Twin Islands. You can't miss Sphinx Rock, a gigantic boulder moved by glacial ice thousands of years ago.

If you're a birdwatcher, the park is a designated Important Bird Area by the National Audubon Society, putting it on an international list of nature parks worth protecting. More than 250 species have been spotted and birds nest in the park year round. The same thought crosses everyone's mind standing on the edge of a tidal pool in Pelham Bay Park: Is this really New York City?

Address Shore Road & Orchard Beach Road, Bronx, NY 10465, +1 (718)430-1891, www.pelhambaypark.org | Getting there Subway to Pelham Bay Park (6 train), transfer to bus Bx12 or seasonal beach shuttle bus | Hours Daily 6am–10pm | Tip Go horseback riding in the park at the Bronx Equestrian Center. You can take an hour-long trail ride through the park and experience its full beauty on horseback (9 Shore Road, Bronx, NY 10464, www.nychorse.com).

# 81 Port Morris Clock Tower
*The landmark building with a face on it*

One of the most recognizable landmarks in the South Bronx is the old Estey Piano & Organ Company factory on the corner of Bruckner Boulevard and Lincoln Avenue. In the 19th and early 20th centuries, this area of Port Morris and Mott Haven was the center of piano and organ manufacturing in New York. Estey had the longest life – more than a century – and left behind its 1886 five-story brick building with a distinctive clock tower.

Estey was founded in Brattleboro, Vermont in the 1840s and acquired other manufacturing operations. It was the largest maker of pianos and pump organs in the United States, rivaling Steinway in Queens, with a grand showroom on Fifth Avenue in Manhattan. Over the years, more than 100 piano companies existed in New York, tapping into European immigrant craftsmen and skilled designers. The pianos made their way into the homes and churches across the world.

By the time of World War I, upright pianos and "parlor organs" fell out of favor when the public turned to recorded music in the home. The piano industry barely survived. Estey hung on by making electric keyboards and narrowing its product line. The business folded in the Bronx in the 1970s. The clock tower remained.

The clock itself is a handsome relic of fine craftsmanship, but it stopped ticking many years ago. It is visible from the Harlem River, and it is the most prominent feature of the neighborhood. The building was renovated and converted to apartments in 2002. The clock tower was made a feature of the new space. In 2006, the New York Landmarks Preservation Commission held hearings to designate the building a city landmark. The Commission noted that this was the oldest piano factory in New York, and that this "brick façade building is a well-preserved example of late 19th-century industrial architecture in the American round arch tradition."

**Address** 112 Lincoln Avenue, Bronx, NY 10454 | **Getting there** Subway to 138th Street (4, 5 train) | **Hours** Unrestricted from the outside only | **Tip** The sound of music can still be found in the old factory. Charlie's Bar and Kitchen is on the ground floor. It hosts weekend brunches with hip-hop and Motown performers (112 Lincoln Avenue, Bronx, NY 10454, www.charliesbarkitchen.com).

# 82__The Point

*Pushing creativity and community in Hunts Point*

What is the brightest spot in Hunts Point? It's The Point, a community development group founded in 1993 that offers youth development classes as well as arts and culture programming. It also is a driver for the revitalization of one of the grittiest areas of the city, from advocating for environmental causes to promoting a free Wi-Fi network for the peninsula community. For almost 25 years, The Point has had a collaborative project with the International Center of Photography. Students are taught the fundamentals of black-and-white photography and use the site's darkroom. The Point opened its Vantage Point Gallery to showcase the work.

The Point offers courses in art, music, and theater to the community. There are adult acting classes in its Open Hydrant Theater, a not-for-profit ensemble. Anyone dreaming of running away and joining the circus can get properly trained here first. Acrobatics, aerial, clowning, and juggling are part of the Cirque du Vie troop. A visual arts workshop brings in accomplished artists and sculptors to teach a variety of mediums. Musicians provide training in the foundation of music theory and the basics of working in a recording studio. All the programs lead to public performances, exhibitions, concerts, and gallery shows. The Point is also the HQ for TATS Cru, the legendary street art creators who have murals seemingly everywhere across the city.

For many years, The Point has been a supporter of the Fish Parade, held annually in June. The parade begins at Hunts Point Riverside Park and winds its way across the peninsula to Barretto Point Park. The parade ends with a salsa music concert and street fair. The Point is making an impact on the peninsula and is helping to not just revitalize the area but foster community development. Attending one of The Point's activities is a good way to learn and support what it is doing.

**Address** 940 Garrison Avenue, Bronx, NY 10474, +1 (718)542-4139, www.thepoint.org | **Getting there** Subway to Hunts Point Avenue (6 train), or bus Bx6, Bx6+ to Hunts Point Avenue / Seneca Avenue | **Hours** Mon–Thu 9am–5pm | **Tip** Explore the neighborhood street art with a map and tour of the Environmental Justice and Public Art Walk. Some of the eight street art murals are clustered around the Point's Riverside Campus (1391 Lafayette Avenue, Bronx, NY 10474).

# 83 Pregones Theater

*Bringing Latino culture to the stage*

The Pregones Theater is one of the leading places in the country showcasing new Latino dance, film, music, and stage performances. The artist-run company recently merged with the beloved Puerto Rican Traveling Theater (PRTT) to form a new partnership to further support emerging artists. Pregones, launched in 1979, and PRTT, in 1967, both have their roots in bringing culture "to the streets" to audiences who would not necessarily be drawn into a traditional theater. Today, the humble-looking theater one block off the Grand Concourse is considered one of the driving forces in presenting Latino culture onstage.

In the 1980s, Pregones was a group of performers traveling together to bring Latino performances around the East Coast. Led by Rosalba Rolón and other dedicated artists, Pregones is now approaching 100 theater premiers and has hosted more than 350 visiting artists. For its South Bronx home, the theater took over a refrigeration equipment factory built in the 1930s. In 2004, demolition and renovation commenced, and what resulted was a 124-seat theater without any obstructions. PRTT has a 50-year reputation in the theater world. One of the greatest Latino actors of all time, Raul Julia, was an early member of PRTT when it launched in the 1960s. Actress Miriam Colón starred with Julia, and she led the theater group to bring bilingual productions to audiences. PRTT played a part in launching the careers of scores of professionals and is always on the lookout for talented emerging playwrights.

The programming is lively. The first Wednesday of the month, free film screenings and discussions are held; the filmmakers participate in a Q&A. The theater hosts concerts, dramas, musicals, and solo performance shows. The visiting artists series brings international professionals to perform, and the theater is a gathering place for friends and family.

Address 575 Walton Avenue, Bronx, NY 10451, +1 (718)585-1202, www.pregonesprtt.org |
Getting there Subway to 149th Street–Grand Concourse (2, 4 train) | Hours Mon–Fri
9:30am–5:30pm, check website for weekend schedule | Tip The organization also
participates in Stage Garden Rumba on spring and summer weekends at Willis Avenue
Community Gardens. Enjoy dance, poetry, and music that celebrates Latino culture
(378 Willis Avenue, Bronx, NY 10454, www.nyrp.org/green-spaces/garden-details/
willis-avenue-community-garden).

# 84__Ralph Lauren Home

*Before Polo, there was baseball*

Look in the closet of your house and more than likely you'll find something to wear that came from Ralph Lauren. Jackets, jeans, shirts, sweaters, and more. For 50 years, his brand has dominated the sportswear market and he has created a fashion empire. No other modern-day Bronx rags-to-riches tale comes even close to his. According to Forbes, Ralph Lauren is worth around $6 billion.

He was born Ralph Lifshitz, the son of an Ashkenazi Jewish immigrant house painter in 1939. One of Lauren's homes was at 3220 Steuben Avenue in the Norwood section of the Bronx. As a teenager, the money he made in after-school jobs was spent on suits. Today he is a collector of rare autos but as a boy he didn't own a bicycle. He played sandlot baseball and was a diehard Yankees fan, sitting in the bleachers with his friends watching Whitey Ford and Mickey Mantle. At 16, he changed his name because kids teased him about it and not, he has said, to hide his Jewish identity. Lauren graduated from DeWitt Clinton High and clerked at Brooks Brothers. He was drafted, sent to Fort Dix for basic training, and served in the US Army from 1962 through 1964. Upon discharge, he resumed his life in New York. As the Manhattan fashion scene exploded in the 1960s, Lauren became a for-hire designer to a tie maker. He founded his own brand, Polo Fashions, in 1968.

"People ask, 'How can a Jewish kid from the Bronx do preppy clothes? Does it have to do with class and money?' It has to do with dreams," he said in the *International Herald Tribune*. He went back to the Bronx to celebrate the 50th anniversary of his company. Lauren threw out the first pitch at Yankee Stadium. "One thing about growing up in the Bronx, you're living a life that's sort of disappeared on a few levels," he told the *Post*. "And it was a very happy life for me. I liked my childhood. I liked my friends."

Address 3220 Steuben Avenue, Bronx, NY 10467 | Getting there Subway to Mosholu Parkway (4 train) | Hours Unrestricted from the outside only | Tip Two blocks away from Ralph Lauren's house was the childhood home of another successful designer, Calvin Klein. They never crossed paths as boys (3191 Rochambeau Avenue, Bronx, NY 10467).

# 85 — Rambling House

*A pub of heroic proportions*

Rambling House is the Irish bar of your dreams. It is a sprawling building holding untold numbers of taps, kegs, and bottles of beer. At one time, the surrounding area was full of Irish-Americans and pubs to serve the incoming immigrants. The area has shrunk somewhat but is no less a vibrant and culturally rich place to visit.

At the helm of Rambling House is a legend in the local bar scene, Joe Carty. The Emerald Isle Immigration Center honors three Irish-Americans annually, and this Woodlawn Heights pub owner was tapped in 2009 for his work supporting the community in the Bronx. Joe is the oldest of six children in a family from Aughavas, County Leitrim. He took a circuitous route to co-ownership of one of the borough's largest pubs. Joe came to New York in 1970 but then left to work on the Alaskan pipeline for five years. After a circuitous route from Ireland back to New York, he's been a fixture here for three decades. Once the sleepy Tara Hill, the bar was transformed in 2003 into Rambling House, a mega-size tavern of taps and TV screens. Regulars refer to it as "The House," and it has a homey vibe. It's a gathering spot for the Irish diaspora and their friends with a mix of live music and DJs five days a week. The Sunday music series begins at 9pm and brings traditional Irish performers that will make you believe you're on the Ring of Kerry. From the kitchen comes a variety of Irish and other dishes such as steak salad, whole-wheat penne pesto, Gaelic chicken, and Irish lamb stew. Rambling House is renowned for its most popular meal, the full Irish breakfast of eggs, rashers, sausages, black pudding, white pudding, baby tomatoes, and mushrooms.

While there has been development in the area and Katonah Avenue has seen many changes, the heart of this stretch of the Bronx is the lively and friendly pubs, and Rambling House is the grandest of all.

Address 4292 Katonah Avenue, Bronx, NY 10470, +1 (718)798-4510, www.ramblinghousenyc.com | Getting there Subway to 233rd Street (2, 5 train), or Metro-North to Woodlawn (Harlem Line) | Hours Daily 11–4am | Tip Stroll along the nearby Bronx River to visit the bucolic Muskrat Cove. This unexpected spot of nature is on the pathway skirting the river underneath the highway overpass and within sight of the Woodlawn Metro-North train platform (4202-4288 Webster Avenue, Bronx, NY 10470).

# 86_Riverdale Diner

*Comfort food served right up*

For five decades, the hard-working staff at the Riverdale Diner have made it the neighborhood eatery of choice for a Reuben or B.L.T. With the neighborhood changing from Irish and Italian to Spanish, the classic diner menu has given way to add fare such as *pernil con ajo* (roast pork with garlic) and the breakfast favorite, *chorizo con huevos* with mangú (smoked Spanish sausage, scrambled with eggs, and served on a hero with plantains). Owners George and Anna Kaperonis run the establishment. You can usually find them sitting in the front of the restaurant, greeting regular customers and watching the diners come and go. George and Anna have been together for more than 60 years ever since George arrived from Greece. "Everyone is welcome here," Anna says. "Now try a German apple pancake!"

The interior has the feel of a mob movie and if it looks familiar that's because it's been used in a dozen TV series. This is the second restaurant on the spot. The Kaperonis tore down their original building in 1985 and built an entirely new diner in its place. They preserve the warm and friendly 1980s vibe. There is plenty of booth space, counter seating, and lots of shiny stainless steel. It also has free parking, which is a rarity in Riverdale.

Anna hints that there's a secret recipe for the diner's chicken szechuan over yellow rice ("I can't say what's in it, but it's good, try it," she says). The number one favorite drink at the bar is also famous in the neighborhood, a frozen Hennessy cognac colada. "Everyone loves them," Anna says. "Try it." The diner does all of its baking on the premises, such as the toasted challah bread used in the meatloaf sandwich. Looking over the menu, Anna points to dishes not typically found in Greek diners, such as the Dominican Republic red bean soup, *sopa de habichuelas rojas*. "Our food is for everyone, that's what makes us special," she says.

**Address** 3657 Kingsbridge Avenue, Bronx, NY 10463, +1 (718)884-6050,
www.riverdalediner.org, info@riverdalediner.com | **Getting there** Subway to 238th Street
(1 train), or bus Bx3, Bx9 to Broadway/West 238th Street | Hours Daily 6am–midnight,
Fri & Sat 6–1am | **Tip** Is Hudson University in Riverdale? No, the fictional school of
*Law & Order: Special Victims Unit* films at the College of Mount St. Vincent. The private
Catholic women's college, opened in 1911, was also used for scenes in *The Blacklist*, *Doubt*,
and *Girls* (6301 Riverdale Avenue, Bronx, NY 10471, www.mountsaintvincent.edu).

# 87 — Riverdale's Boldface Names

*Lifestyles of the rich and famous*

Riverdale is the neighborhood with the biggest collection of ritzy old homes in the borough. This area has, for generations, been the home of boldface names, from singers to movie stars to mayors and future presidents. The homes boast a variety of architectural styles, and from the curb, a wide array of designs is evident.

In the 19th century, developers carved up the rocky landscape overlooking the Hudson River. It was no good for farming but great for building mansions. Country homes were erected by wealthy Manhattanites. One called his house the "incubator" for continuing the family line. There are a large number of single-family homes today along with luxury co-ops and condos.

Among the famous to reside here was Ella Fitzgerald, who as a teen briefly lived at the Colored Orphan Asylum, today the Hebrew Home at Riverdale, 5901 Palisade Avenue. Following three consecutive terms as mayor of New York City, Fiorello La Guardia bought an English Tudor at 5020 Goodridge Avenue and died in the house in 1947. Yankees' first baseman Lou Gehrig drove to the stadium from his family home at 5204 Delafield Avenue. When Joseph Kennedy was living with his family at 5040 Independence Avenue from 1927–1929, future president John F. Kennedy was a schoolboy at nearby Riverdale Country School.

Riverdale is an enjoyable neighborhood to walk in. It's hilly and heavily wooded, and the best time to visit is the fall and winter when the leaves have fallen and you can see the hidden homes. There are few sidewalks and many "Private Road" signs. You can still walk down the road – "Private road" only means they are not maintained by the city. The homes in Fieldston and scenery around Ploughmans Bush are particularly noteworthy.

Address Near the intersection of Henry Hudson Parkway and West 246th Street, Bronx, NY 10471 | Getting there Bus Bx7, Bx10, Bx20 to Henry Hudson Parkway/West 246th Street | Hours Unrestricted | Tip A secret park is located at the dead end of Livingston Avenue in Fieldston. Delafield Park is privately owned, but unlike Gramercy Park, you don't need a key to visit, just walking shoes. Indian Pond is the small serene spot in the middle. It's only accessible by foot as only Fieldston residents are allowed to park cars (Livingston Avenue and West 246th Street, Bronx, NY 10471).

# 88__Shamrock IV Yacht Mast

*From noble America's Cup contender to flagstaff*

On a tiny hill on Bronx Community College is a piece of an America's Cup racing yacht surrounded by century-old artillery pieces. All are decaying on what was known as Battery Hill during the American Revolution.

Sir Thomas Lipton (1851–1931) was a self-made millionaire as a grocery store owner in Victorian England. Lipton Tea brought him immense wealth. He poured his money into trying to win the America's Cup. In five fruitless attempts, he sunk $10 million (about $163 million today) to win a $500 trophy. His fourth attempt was in July 1920 with *Shamrock IV*, which narrowly lost to *Resolute*. Lipton loved the Bronx. Five months before the race, a ferocious fire tore through City Island's shipyard, destroying many pricey racing yachts. But FDNY Engine 70 saved the *Shamrock IV*, and Lipton became a friend of the firehouse.

Five years after the race, Lipton had the yacht dismantled. He donated the mast to the Bronx, and during commencement ceremonies in 1925 dedicated it to New York University students who served in World War I. It was converted into a radio antenna and flagpole. The steel section is 113 feet long and a topmast of wood is 56 feet. Sadly, it has deteriorated badly and no flag tops the flagstaff.

Placed around it are five vintage weapons. Why? Marshal Ferdinand Foch, commander in chief of the Allies, toured New York in 1921. NYU awarded him an honorary Doctor of Law degree, and Foch presented a captured German cannon to the school. Somehow, it escaped the Word War II scrap metal drives. There are also two German artillery pieces, a 7.7cm FK 16 Feldkanone and 15cm sFH 13 Howitzer, a British Armstrong-Whitworth quick-firing gun, a US Navy 3"/50 caliber deck gun, and a Civil War-era 13-inch Union Seacoast Mortar model from 1861. When NYU sold the campus in 1973, it left behind these and other memorials.

Address Carl Polowczyk Hall, Bronx, NY 10453, +1 (718)289-5100 | Getting there Subway to Burnside Avenue (Line 4), Metro-North to University Heights, or bus Bx3 to 181th Street | Hours Mon–Fri 9am–5pm, Sat & Sun 10am–4pm | Tip For authentic Mexican food and delicious tacos, trek to Taco's El Paisanito. This tiny spot has spicy homemade dishes and a friendly staff (202 West Fordham Road, Bronx, NY 10468, www.tacoselpaisanitosbronxny.com).

# 89__Shine Sneaker Store
*Where the cognoscenti tread for Jordans*

Michael Jordan said, "It's not about the shoes, it's about what you do in them. It's about being who you are born to be." The NBA Hall of Famer could be talking directly to the Marble Hill kids who flock to Shine in the shadow of the elevated 1 train. They line up for exclusives and new releases that are piled high in the brightly lit sneaker boutique.

There has been a shoe store in the location for more than two decades, but brothers Paul and David Kim launched Shine in the space in August 2018. Retail is in their blood. Their dad had a clothing store on the Grand Concourse for more than 35 years, and as kids they grew up working there and learning the business. They can still rely on him for advice and counsel as they made moves to strike out on their own and remodel their store. Shine quickly built up a following among the local sneakerheads.

The goal for the brothers was to build a sneaker emporium that brought Manhattan to Marble Hill, a place for the neighborhood to know that they were going to stock the hottest brands. While some run to $250 a pair, they also stock kicks for kids at more modest prices. They carry all the popular neighborhood brands, ASICS, New Balance, Nike, and Jordans, from toddlers to adult sizes.

"We want to stay current with our product and be known as a trendsetting store, not following trends," Paul said. "Everyone wants exclusives, and we try to carry shoes that others don't. I'll open the store at 10 on a Saturday morning, and there have been people waiting in line since 3am for releases. Jordans release on Saturdays, Michael Jordan doesn't want kids to ditch school to wait for releases, so no one skips school."

Shine counts on the neighborhood for store traffic, but out-of-towners are starting to find out about it. "We want to bring the boutique level feel," Paul says. Shine is making strides in that direction.

Address 5537 Broadway, Bronx, NY 10463, +1 (718)549-3260, www.shinebx.com | Getting there Subway to Marble Hill–225th Street (1 train) | Hours Mon–Sat 10am–8pm, Sun noon–6pm | Tip Walk over the nearby Broadway Bridge to Manhattan, and you'll have the Harlem River underneath you and the 1 train above you. Start at 225th Street (www.nycroads.com/crossings/broadway).

# 90 __ Slave Burial Ground
*Civil rights history*

Public School 48, an elementary school in Hunts Point, played a part in the documentation of a long-forgotten burial ground where the remains of slaves are interred. The school neighbors Drake Park, which was once an estate with a private cemetery; P.S. 48 is named Joseph R. Drake School after a young doctor and poet interred in the park. Archeologists and historians guide the fourth- and fifth-grade students to study the small park's lost graves of nearly 50 slaves.

Less than 10 years ago, the burial ground was completely forgotten. In 2014, Philip Panaritis, a retired Bronx educator whose specialty is history and urban archeology, discovered a circa-1910 photo in the collection of the Museum of the City of New York. It was marked on the reverse with "Slave Burying Ground Hunts Point Road." He deduced it was across the road from the cemetery that is today in Drake Park that contains the men and women who were the 17th-century slave owners.

The last burial in the Slave Burial Ground occurred around 1840. All of the burials were men and women who were the property of area landowners before slavery was outlawed in New York in 1827. Among them were a blacksmith, coachmen, drovers, cooks, farm laborers, and wood cutters. Panaritis and P.S. 48 teacher Justin Czarka launched the Hunts Point Slave Burial Ground Project to document and educate the surrounding community about this important piece of history in the middle of their neighborhood. The school children use the cemetery as a part of their history curriculum, visiting it, studying it, and working with the city and state to get it landmark status. There are no grave markers for the former slaves, and the community wishes to honor them. A visit today is to the open field next to the gated, whites-only cemetery. The long-term dream of the community is to create a memorial monument.

**Address** Oakpoint Avenue, between Hunts Point Avenue, Longfellow Avenue, and Drake Street, Bronx, NY 10474 | **Getting there** Bus Bx6 to Halleck Street/Oakpoint Avenue | **Hours** Daily 6am–10pm | **Tip** Get your coffee at nearby Boogie Down Grind Café, known for its ambiance and beloved community meeting point. In addition to grinding beans, the shop has open mic nights, karaoke, and pop-up art shows. Go for a Bombon – espresso and condensed milk topped with whipped cream and chocolate drizzle (866 Hunts Point Avenue, Bronx, NY 10474, www.boogiedowngrind.com).

# 91 Sonia Sotomayor Mural

*The Soundview honors a beloved daughter*

In acting, it's an Oscar or a Tony Award. But the ultimate honor in Soundview is a wall mural painted by the top area street artists. This is the tribute in paint for the most talked-about former resident, Justice Sonia Sotomayor, who is the first Hispanic US Supreme Court Justice.

Alfredo Oyague (aka Per One) gathered fellow artists from FX and TATS Cru in 2015 to create the mural. He secured a spot at Morrison and Westchester Avenues. It depicts other local heroes and a streetscape of neighborhood life. Justice Sotomayor, standing 12 feet high in her black robes, is an inspiring sight. Sotomayor even attended the unveiling to the delight of the crew that created the mural. She appeared tickled at the honor, and in brief remarks reminisced about her girlhood growing up in the Bronxdale Houses.

Her parents were immigrants from Puerto Rico who moved the family to Soundview in the 1950s in search of a better life. At 8, young Sonia was diagnosed with diabetes, and at 9 her father died of heart disease. Her mother supported two kids on a nurse's salary to put her through Blessed Sacrament School. This prepared her for Cardinal Spellman High where she was valedictorian. She was in a small minority at Princeton where she wrote her senior thesis on Luis Muñoz Marín. Sotomayor dedicated it in part "to the people of my island – for the rich history that is mine." Her career trajectory from assistant district attorney to private practice and onto the federal court was practically meteoric. In 2009, President Obama nominated her for the Supreme Court.

In her autobiography *My Beloved World*, she writes, "There are uses to adversity, and they don't reveal themselves until tested," she says. "Whether it's serious illness, financial hardship, or the simple constraint of parents who speak limited English, difficulty can tap unsuspected strengths."

Address Morrison and Westchester Avenues, Bronx, NY 10472 | Getting there Subway to Elder Avenue (6 train) | Hours Unrestricted | Tip Walk east to visit Concrete Plant Park on the Bronx River. It was created on the site of an abandoned industrial zone. Today, it is a landscaped greenway for biking, fishing, running, and walking (1040 Sheridan Expressway, Bronx, NY 10459, www.nycgovparks.org/parks/concrete-plant-park).

# 92 _ South Bronx Farmers Market

*Bringing fresh produce to the public*

With one million square feet of space, Hunts Point Terminal Market handles 210 million packages of produce every year, but only a relatively small portion ends up in Bronx kitchens. Entrepreneurs Roseanne Placencia and Lily Kesselman wanted to change that and get fresh produce into the borough's bellies. The pair launched the South Bronx Farmers Market in 2016 to bring fresh, locally grown produce to Mott Haven.

Located along East 138th Street between Willis and Alexander Avenues, the venture launched with a modest grant from the Citizens Committee of New York. City Farms Markets, a network of community-run farmers markets, is a partner. It was an immediate hit in the area and lived up to its mission "to address the public health crises in obesity, diabetes, malnourishment, and undernourishment by promoting access to nutritious, affordable, locally grown produce and related agricultural products for the underserved residents of the South Bronx."

Among the most popular items are apples, basil, cilantro (Chinese parsley), eggs, kale, peppers, onions, squash, sunflower honey, and tea. The operation is run by a non-profit, the South Bronx Farmers Market, Inc., from June through November.

For those interested in farm-to-table, you'll find a variety of regional farmers popular in markets across the city. Unique to the borough, there are also hyper-local vendors growing produce and selling at the market. These include La Finca del Sur, offering Bronx-grown herbs, vegetables, and flowers, and Sky Vegetables, a Bronx-based hydroponic farm on the roof of a building on Tinton Avenue. Through the market, vendors are supporting the mission of bringing healthy food to the community by accepting payment via various food assistance programs.

Address East 138th Street between Willis and Alexander Avenues, Bronx, NY 10454, www.southbronxfarmersmarket.com, southbronxfarmersmarket@gmail.com | **Getting there** Subway to Third Avenue – 138th Street (6 train) | **Hours** June – Nov, Wed & Sat 10am – 4pm | **Tip** The 40th Police Precinct House is a 90-year-old limestone and granite gem in the historic district. A new station for the precinct was built nearby but this building is among the finest for the Finest (257 Alexander Avenue, Bronx, NY 10454).

# 93 __ St. Ann's Founding Fathers

*A house of worship built by a son for his family*

The oldest church still standing in the borough is St. Ann's Episcopal Church in Morrisania. This small house of worship is made of fieldstone and features a Greek Revival-style steeple. Its Gothic stained-glass windows are deeply set and are dedicated to some of the oldest families in the area. St. Ann's is worth visiting to see the simple nature of the building and the historic cemetery next to it. It was a country church set in rolling hills at a time when one family owned a large swath of the Bronx.

St. Ann's was built by Gouverneur Morris II in 1841. He was the wealthy scion of the Morris family, who once controlled all of the land that is now called Morrisania. His father, Gouverneur Morris, was not just his father but also a Founding Father. As a New York senator, he was one of the principal framers of the US Constitution. Historians also believe he wrote the famous preamble to the Constitution, "We the People of the United States, in order to form a perfect Union…"

The prime reason for Gouverneur Morris II to build the church was to create a churchyard to bury famous family members. This is the final resting place of Gouverneur and Ann Morris, Lewis Morris, the first native-born chief justice of New York, and his grandson, also named Lewis Morris, signer of the Declaration of Independence. The church was named St. Ann's after Morris' mother, for whom the church is dedicated, Ann Cary Randolph. She was a distant cousin of Thomas Jefferson and, in what was a bit of a scandal, had once been the family housekeeper.

The church was added to the National Register of Historic Places in 1980. The neighborhood has undergone significant changes over the years and today St. Ann's caters to the needs of a diverse community. It has a longstanding neighborhood outreach program.

Address 295 St. Ann's Avenue, Bronx, NY 10454, +1 (718)585-5632, www.stannssouthbronx.org | Getting there Subway to Brook Avenue (6 train) | Hours The church is open for special events and holidays | Tip Mott Haven clothing designer and impresario Christian Vazquez launched his Famous Nobodys brand in 2017, and it quickly became one of the go-to shop for trendsetters in the South Bronx. His clever designs ("Fast Cash / Never Lasts") are combined with bold colors and dazzling screen-printing (130 Alexander Avenue, Bronx, NY 10454, www.famousnobodys.com).

# 94 __ St. James Tiffany Windows
*Spiritual art in stained glass*

Louis Comfort Tiffany provided stained-glass art for so many customers from the Gilded Age to the Jazz Age that his name is synonymous today with beauty and style. What if you were to learn there was enough Tiffany pieces in one spot to be considered a miniature museum? Fine art has been proudly displayed on Fordham Road in the peaceful little church of St. James Church where six stained-glass windows were created by the son of the founder of Tiffany & Co.

Not every window in the church is by Tiffany. Four are by Henry Sharp and four came from the Royal Bavarian Stained Glass Manufactory in Munich. The Tiffany stained-glass windows are distinctive and easy to find. *The Last Supper* (1889) dates from early in his career and contains many painted sections. In 1895, Tiffany delivered *The True Vine* masterpiece, which intertwines wheat and grapes. Observe *The True Vine* in sunlight to see how three-dimensional it appears and a true sign of Tiffany's artistry. *Lilies and Apple Blossoms* is dedicated to his daughter Julia W. Tiffany, who was married in the church. Look for Tiffany's name on two windows. It is rare to find his signature on his work. Each are dedicated to parishioners and loved ones with Bronx ties.

The Episcopal church was founded in 1853 and parishioners spent decades decorating and finishing the artwork of the Gothic Revival structure. Wealthy Manhattan families owned many country villas in Fordham Heights and University Heights. They needed a place to worship and built St. James in the style of an English country church. While the Bronx changed, the church adapted to the times and today still welcomes all who come to the neighborhood. The Sunday morning service begins at 11am and the liturgy includes music influenced by the members of the church. Afterwards, stay and soak in the beauty of these pieces of American ecclesiastical art.

In tender
and Reverent
Memory ✠ of
Julia Wheeler Tiffany

...of the
Third ✠ Rector
of this Parish

**Address** 2500 Jerome Avenue, Bronx, NY 10468, +1 (718)367-0655,
www.stjamesfordham.org, saintjamesfordham@gmail.com | **Getting there** Subway to
Fordham Road (4, B, D train) | **Hours** See website for seasonal schedule | **Tip** Fordham
Road was once home to many theaters, among more than 100 in the Bronx. Today, the
Bronx County Historical Society offers a trolley tour to visit lost picture houses. The
tour begins in Woodlawn Cemetery with a visit to the graves of movie and stage stars
(www.bronxhistoricalsociety.org).

# 95 __ St. Mary's Park Crash Site

*Aircraft miraculously misses homes and parkgoers*

A tragedy that is seared into the memories of hundreds of residents of the South Bronx is a plane crash in St. Mary's Park. Just a few years after two planes collided over Brooklyn, all six people on board a twin-engine private plane were killed upon impact in front of scores of witnesses in the neighborhood around the park. The plane came down on the afternoon of September 16, 1967, right on top of the "sliding rock" at East 149th Street and Eagle Avenue.

The blue and white Cessna 320 Skyknight departed LaGuardia Airport bound for Cincinnati. At the controls was the 28-year-old pilot, Ronald Bernert, of Hamilton, Ohio. Less than 10 minutes after lifting off in Queens, the plane's engines began to fail. It wobbled over the rooftops and circled low, narrowly missing the Robert E. Moore Houses on Jackson Avenue. It banked sharply towards the hill. At 12:41pm, the plane spun sideways as it struck the hillside, bursting into flame.

In addition to the pilot, the victims included a doctor from Oklahoma along with his wife and mother and other family members and friends. Miraculously, no one on the ground was hurt.

First responders had a difficult time getting through the crowd of gawkers. Firefighters from Ladder 17 battled the flames and Rescue 3 extricated the victims. The six were laid in a row on the hillside under a blanket, and a priest from St. Pius V's Church offered last rites. Pieces of the tail were found on the roof of a house. When the wreckage was removed, the rocks were painted black as a sign of mourning. Investigators later determined the plane was almost 300 pounds overweight.

Ivette Cardona was 10 and watched the crash from Concord Avenue. "My mother and I also ran over there," she recalled. "It was a sight I will never forget. Even as an adult, whenever I passed by that smooth rock I always remember that very sad day on 149th Street."

Address East 149th Street and Eagle Avenue, Bronx, NY 10454 | Getting there Subway to Jackson Avenue (2, 5 train) | Hours Daily 6am–10pm | Tip The public housing that was nearly struck by the plane is the childhood home of baseball superstar Roberto Martin Antonio Bonilla, aka Bobby Bonilla. He would have been four at the time of the crash. His 15-year MLB career is remembered today because the Mets must pay his deferred salary until 2035 (674 East 179th Street, Bronx, NY 10457).

# 96__Stickball Boulevard

*Keeping a beloved pastime alive*

A two-block length of asphalt and pavement is the home turf of the New York Emperors Stickball League, a grassroots organization that keeps alive a faded city childhood tradition in Castle Hill. All it takes to play stickball is a relatively empty street, a broomstick or mop handle, and a rubber high-bounce ball. Fire hydrants and parked cars serve as obstacles, manhole covers are bases. Stickball Boulevard is sandwiched between Lafayette and Randall Avenues and it is closed to traffic for games.

In the 1980s, the league was a hotbed of stickball activity for local teams. The league started in 1985 with two teams and has grown to as many as sixteen. Opening Day is in April and Sunday games follow through August. Tournaments are held on major holidays from Memorial Day to Columbus Day. These are big affairs with DJs pumping out salsa music, BBQ grills, and non-stop games all day. Among the teams in the league are the Bronx Diamondbacks, Emperors, Leland Legends, Silver Bullets, and Sugar Hill.

The street is a living memorial for a firefighter killed in the 9/11 terror attacks. Steve Mercado was 38 and a member of Engine 40. He was also a Little League coach and president of the stickball league. Outside the stickball fence is a mural of Mercado at bat and his poignant poem, written the year he died, which ends:

*Stickball's the game, and each week we play*
*Running, hitting, laughing, enjoying the day*
*Our families, our friends, we love them the same*
*Look forward to seeing you Sunday to play "Our Game."*

One of Mercado's dreams was to launch a youth division so that his two young sons could join him. He didn't live long enough to see this happen, but the league created a boys and girls league after Mercado's death. Today, it is wildly popular and makes stickball a multi-generational sport on the streets. His name is now on Stickball Boulevard.

**Address** Stickball Boulevard and Randall Avenue, Bronx, NY 10473 | **Getting there**
Bus Bx39 to White Plains Road / Randall Avenue | **Hours** Unrestricted | **Tip** Havemeyer
Garden Association partnered with GrowNYC to design a 7,600-square-foot neighborhood
garden on a lot preserved by the fire department. The Castle Hill garden has more than
25 beds, plus benches and picnic tables (535 Havemeyer Avenue, Bronx, NY 10473,
www.grownyc.org/openspace/gardens/bx/havemeyer-garden-association).

# 97__Stockbridge Warriors

*Native Americans fought and died here*

One of the most important Revolutionary War sites in Bronx County is the property around Van Cortlandt Park. George Washington visited (see ch. 101) with his men during the war. Bloody conflict played out in the woods around what is today the South Bronx with skirmishes throughout the late 1770s.

The Stockbridge Native Americans were descendants of the Mohicans who were native to the New York region. When white settlers pushed the Mohicans out, they relocated to what is modern-day Connecticut and Massachusetts. A Christian missionary gathered them into a Mohican village which the English named Stockbridge and called them the Stockbridge Indians. These men and women sided with the colonists during the war for independence.

The Stockbridge warriors wore coarse linen shirts to their knees, linen trousers, deerskin shoes, and hats made of woven plant fibers. They carried muskets, battle-axes, and a quiver of arrows. They fought bravely at all the key battles from Bunker Hill to Monmouth.

On August 31, 1778, the Battle of Van Cortlandt's Woods pitted the US Continental Army, with Stockbridge warriors serving as light infantry, against the loyalist Queen's Rangers and Hessian mercenaries. The odds were against the patriots as they were outnumbered 5 to 1. The battle turned into a rout and the colonists fled. In retreat, the Stockbridge warriors were trapped and massacred. Scores were killed in the battle on the Van Cortlandt property. Locals buried nearly 20 where they fell.

A memorial was erected in 1906 in a location now called Indian Field. It houses a baseball field and bocce courts and the Stockbridge warriors are not actually buried here. They are interred several hundred yards away in a spot reached by walking along the footpath toward the park nursery. To the left of the lane past the nursery is an open field in the forest, and this is the true burial spot.

Address 4222 Van Cortlandt Park East, Bronx, NY 10470, +1 (718)430-1890, www.vcpark.org/the-park/features/34-fields/62-indian-field.html | **Getting there** Subway to Woodlawn (6 train) | **Hours** Daily dawn–dusk | Tip Get wet and try not to tip your canoe over at the nearby Shoelace Park Kayak Launch. Located on the Bronx River, you can launch your own canoe or kayak (East 219th Street and Bronx Boulevard, Bronx, NY 10467, www.nycgovparks.org/facilities/kayak/43).

# 98 Terranova Bakery

*Loaves made with love*

Does anything smell better than freshly baked bread? Step in the doors of Terranova Bakery, which has been turning out fresh loaves for over 50 years. It is one of the most popular destinations of any Arthur Avenue food exploration. Arthur Avenue is an area of Belmont lined with numerous delicious places to eat and buy food.

Shop for the traditional Italian breads baked on the premises. They include *pane di casa* (home bread, which regulars take to calling Terranova Bread), whole wheat, *ciabatta* (flat bread made with olive oil) and *cicolo*, which is the same bread the Romans favored. The types of specialty breads Terranova bakes reflect the diverse neighborhood. Some of them you won't find in Italy. They make challah, Irish soda bread, multigrain, olive, raisin and walnut, rosemary, sourdough, and a whole-wheat loaf that's immensely popular. The shop sells multigrain dough for customers who want to make pizza at home.

Sicilian immigrant Pietro "Peter" Terranova launched the business in the 1960s. Along with his brother, Gandolfo, they built up the business, expanded into wholesale operations, and added to the store. With their wives Vera and Mina, they created a go-to destination in the busy Little Italy section of Belmont. With the changing demographics of the area, it isn't only Italians who shop and work at Terranova. The largely Latin American staff now make and sell the popular products, and a steady stream of customers tend to speak Spanish and not Italian. A new generation of Terranova family members stepped into the business and run it today.

Many bakeries might think that bread isn't important anymore, but Terranova keeps those loaves coming out of the oven. At all of the major religious holidays, lines of customers form to get the perfect bread for big family gatherings. The golden perfect crust comes out, slips into a bag or box, and you're waiting on the ecstasy that only comes from biting into a fresh piece of baked goodness.

Address 691 East 187th Street, Bronx, NY 10458, +1 (718)367-6985, www.terranovabakery.com, info@terranovabakery.com | **Getting there** Subway to Pelham Parkway (2, 5 train), transfer to bus Bx12 heading west to East Fordham Road/ Hoffman Street. Walk south on Arthur Avenue. | **Hours** Mon–Sat 6:30am–6pm, Sun 6am–2:30pm | **Tip** The way to experience Belmont's Little Italy is on a guided culinary tour. Multiple licensed guides offer tours, who are members of the Guides Association of New York City. Consult their list to find one who is right for you and arrive hungry (www.ganyc.org/find-guide).

# 99___Tuff City Styles Tattoos
*Where ink and graffiti influence each other*

For skin art enthusiasts, getting inked in the Bronx has long meant going through the doors of Tuff City Styles across the street from Fordham. It was launched in 1993 – four years before the city resumed licensing tattooists – by graffiti artists and has the vibe of a hangout for street art fanatics. For more than 10 years, the studio has been in a location that has ample outdoor wall space for visiting graffiti artists to express themselves. It's the oldest and busiest tattoo shop in the Bronx.

There are 10 staff artists, and guest inkers drop in from around the world. If there's one consistent element to Tuff City Styles' work, it's that it is always reliably eye-catching. The artists cover the gamut of styles. The traditional styles with bright colors and bold lines are still popular. Classic realism of faces and illustrations stand out, with a lot of celebrities and family members making an appearance. Animals, crosses, and flowers are always popular. The shop also offers piercings, and they can pierce any body part. For artists working on different kinds of canvases, the shop stocks a wide variety of paints and art supplies.

The interior of the shop is carefully designed with the signature element. Four replica R22 subway trains (Numbers 1, 4, 5, and 7, of course) serve as private tattoo artist workspaces. Tuff City Styles owner Joel Brick (aka Med), who still tattoos by appointment, set the store up to be street art Mecca. It hosts events, has been used in music videos, and has a professional recording studio. If you're lucky, you'll spot one of the many celebrities from the world of music who are customers.

One side of the building has a full-scale mock-up of a modern subway car. It's always painted, and bombers showcase their style on it. When you make return visits, the old mural will be replaced with a new one. On the sides of the yard are other, smaller walls on which to paint murals, and artists from around the world visit to tag the walls.

Address 650 East Fordham Road, Bronx, NY 10458, +1 (718)563-4157, www.tuffcitystyles.com, tuffcity@aol.com | Getting there Subway to Fordham Road (B, D train) | Hours Wed–Sun noon–midnight | Tip If you get tattoos in the style of Cardi B, why not also go to her nail salon? The singer gets her nails done by Jenny Bui at Nails on Seventh (305 East Fordham Road, Bronx, NY 10458, www.jennysecret.net).

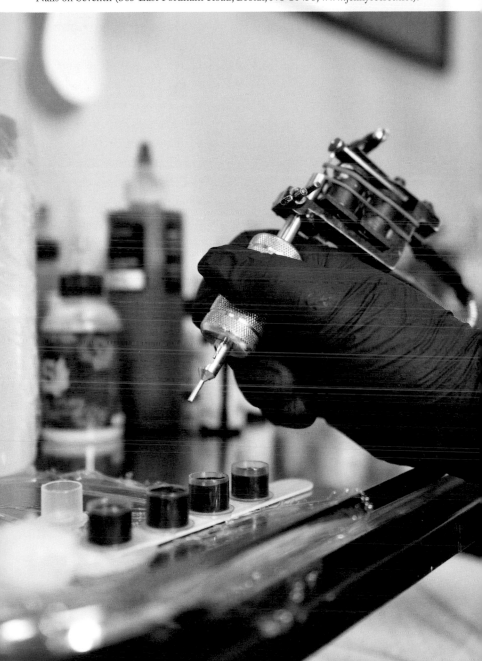

# 100 Valentine-Varian House

*The Revolution was here if these walls could talk*

In 1758, when there was wheat and not concrete in the Bronx – and it was Redcoats not Red Sox that were despised – a simple stone house was built that would go on to play a part in the American Revolution. This is the Valentine-Varian House, one of the fifteen oldest buildings in the five boroughs, and the second oldest home in the Bronx.

Farmer and blacksmith Isaac Valentine built the two-story cut fieldstone house on property purchased from the Dutch Reformed Church. When you look at it from the front, you can see the symmetrical style with matching chimneys at either end of the house. Inside, a central hallway in the middle evenly divides the rooms. But this isn't just any old house. It was caught on the frontlines as skirmishes between the British Army and Continental Army raged around it; six battles were fought on the property. The Valentine family was evicted as the home was taken over by American, British, and Hessian mercenaries. Did George Washington sleep here? Probably not. But his friends did.

After Valentine's fortunes reversed, he was forced to sell the house and farm. Farmer and butcher Isaac Varian took over the 260-acre farm (of what is partially present-day Williams Bridge) around 1792. His family held onto it for the rest of the 19th century. Subsequent owners maintained it well enough that in 1965 it was donated to the Bronx County Historical Society. They moved it across the street and turned it sideways.

In 1966, the Landmarks Preservation Commission designated the house a New York City Landmark, calling attention to "its important qualities… a fine but simple example of Georgian domestic architecture solidly constructed of good materials." Today, it is home of the Museum of Bronx History. Changing exhibits tell the story of the area. When visiting, be sure to take a guided tour and note the original details preserved for over 260 years.

Address 3266 Bainbridge Avenue, Bronx, NY 10467, +1 (718)881-8900, www.bronxhistoricalsociety.org, administration@bronxhistoricalsociety.org | Getting there Subway to East 205th Street (D train) | Hours Sat 10am–4pm, Sun 1–5pm | Tip Directly behind the house is the Williamsbridge Oval. At one time a reservoir, today it's a huge flat expanse of grass and open field. Lace up your running shoes and hit the Olympic-quality track (3225 Reservoir Oval East, Bronx, NY 10467, www.nycgovparks.org/parks/williamsbridge-oval).

# 101 Van Cortlandt House

*George Washington ate here*

Enter the oldest dining room in the borough, where generals Lafayette, Rochambeau, and Washington ate during the American Revolution. General Washington also spent the night here during his peripatetic Army campaign. This is Van Cortlandt House, built in 1748. It is the oldest building in the Bronx.

The home was built for the family of Frederick Van Cortlandt on a wheat farm his family had owned since 1691, one of the earliest agriculture businesses. By the time of the American Revolution the area was sparsely populated. The roadway to Manhattan passed in front of the property and the region was the scene of much bloodshed. Both the British and the Americans occupied the home; even Washington's foe, General William Howe, lived here (see ch. 11). In the 19th century, the Van Cortlandt family sold the home and property to the city for a park and museum. Around the same time, the city was gifted a herd of bison – and who could turn down such a fine gift – which were put to pasture in Van Cortlandt Park. The herdsmen lived in the house. Ultimately, the buffalo were sent to the Bronx Zoo, and their keepers were sent packing.

Realizing the home's historic nature, the National Society of Colonial Dames in the State of New York restored the manor in 1896, creating a museum of 18th-century life. They have been the caretakers and stewards ever since, under an agreement with the NYC Parks Department. Over the years, items have come back to the house from descendants. Today it's a national landmark inside and out, and is the first historic house museum in New York City. The Dames manage the property. Admire the furniture and decorative arts in the public rooms, from the tiles over the fireplace to the period furnishings. The dining room is particularly stunning. This home is where great leaders of the American Revolution rested, and where buffalo once roamed in the Bronx.

**Address** 6036 Broadway, Van Cortlandt Park, Bronx, NY 10471, +1 (718)543-3344, www.vchm.org | **Getting there** Subway to 242nd Street (1 train) | **Hours** Tue–Fri 10am–4pm, Sat & Sun 11am–4pm | **Tip** A short walk away is Lloyd's Carrot Cake, a third-generation family bakery that has served the community's sweet tooth for almost 30 years. Go for the cake – the red velvet, German-chocolate, and pineapple-coconut cakes are beloved staples (6087 Broadway, Bronx, NY 10471, www.lloydscarrotcake.com).

# 102 — Van Cortlandt Golf Course

*The club with a heart in the park*

The first public golf course in the United States is the beautiful 18-hole Van Cortlandt Park Golf Course. The first municipal links came about after a petition was started by sportsmen, to create a course on public land that would be open to all. Female players would be welcomed a few years later in the era. Nine holes were built in 1895 with the remainder opening a few years later. Newspapers took note and this helped to advertise the game. The course was a smashing success, and cities across the country opened their own municipal courses, spurring the growth of golf before World War I. *Golf Digest*, the bible for golfers, named the course as one of the most important in the sport. It credits the course as the place where concepts were invented that players take for granted today, such as booking advance tee times.

Players say they like the back nine the most, and you may think you're playing upstate. The holes are not very long and the course layout receives good reviews. The course has had a long list of celebrity players over the decades. In the early 1930s, Bing Crosby and Bob Hope spent their free time on the vaudeville circuit playing together at Van Cortlandt. Something about the game brought the Three Stooges here. The clubhouse was a hangout for baseball stars Willie Mays, Jackie Robinson, and Babe Ruth. The 18th hole is named "Wall Street" for the 1987 movie filmed at the course.

After falling on hard times and looking ragged around the edges, the club received a multimillion dollar refurbishment around 2007. Greens were replaced and drainage systems improved. The Edwardian-style clubhouse was renovated and expanded with a deck overlooking the lake next door. Van Cortlandt Park regained some of its stature. Today, it's one of the busiest in the state, and is open year-round depending on the weather.

**Address** 115 Van Cortlandt Park South, Bronx, NY 10471, +1 (718)543-4595, www.nycgovparks.org/parks/VanCortlandtPark/facilities/golf | Getting there Subway to Van Cortlandt Park—242nd Street (1 train) | Hours  Check website for schedule and tee times | Tip Overlooking the lake is the club restaurant, the Lake House. The café has a full bar and restaurant open to the public, not only golfers (115 Van Cortlandt Park South, Bronx, NY 10471, www.vancortlandtlakehouse.com).

# 103__Veterans Museum
*A funeral home honors lost veterans*

There are certain things you expect to see when one pays their respects at a funeral home. In addition to the deceased, there may be flowers, mourners, and photos. However, in a stately Morris Park funeral home, you will find a small, poignant museum dedicated to the nation's veterans, created by former soldiers and sailors themselves. Visit John Dormi and Sons Funeral Home to see the Bronx Veterans Museum. Founded in 1999, the museum has humble roots. A coffee shop was the gathering place for local veterans. The funeral home staff also stopped in for their coffee. When a small display the vets created for a library needed a new home, they asked if the funeral home would be interested in housing it. Soon, the funeral home was the destination of rare items you'd expect to see in a historical society.

World War II Navy Seabee Joseph Garofalo was the founder. Word spread, families attending funerals took notice, and the museum quickly received more donations. Today, every conflict going back to the Civil War is represented. Objects include artillery pieces and bullet molds from the 1860s, plastic models, mess kits, captured Japanese knives, a 1917 flare pistol, swords, and medals galore. There are big, thick binders with pages of data on Bronx veterans. A complete Vietnam War POW uniform and sandals is near a helicopter pilot helmet. There's an amazing collection of dog tags, helmets, and gas masks.

The funeral home, managed by Vietnam veteran Chris DiCostanzo, Jr., welcomes the attention. They lovingly maintain the items which fill up display cases and cover walls. Model planes hang from the ceiling. Annually, fifth graders from P.S. 108 troop come over to examine the collection and learn a little US history. The school took Garofalo to heart and held his funeral here when he passed away in 2016. A tree memorial in his honor stands in front of the school.

**Address** 1121 Morris Park Avenue, Bronx, NY 10461, +1 (718)863-2000, www.dignitymemorial.com/funeral-homes/bronx-ny/john-dormi-sons/7315 | **Getting there** Subway to Morris Park (5 train) | **Hours** Mon–Sat 10am–5pm | **Tip** After learning about real heroes, step into the world of fantasy and comic book superheroes at The Lair. With Batman co-created in the Bronx (see ch. 63) here's the place to fill up on back issues and new releases or pick up Gotham City swag (1808 Colden Avenue, Bronx, NY 10462, www.laironline.net).

# 104__Virginia Poe Deathbed

*A sad chapter in the life of the macabre master*

Edgar Allan Poe has a small but notable footprint in the Bronx. His cottage has been visited for more than 100 years as a museum, and the park around it is known to all. Before he was a world-famous author and poet, he was a struggling writer living here with his beloved wife, who was slowly succumbing to a fatal illness.

Born to actors in 1809, Poe struggled to establish himself as a young man. He was schooled in England and the US and wrote in his spare time. We worked to become a man of letters with little early success. Poe had a brief career in the US Army but he was expelled from West Point in 1831 and moved to Baltimore to reside with his aunt Maria Clemm and her daughter Virginia. Poe was publishing poetry at the time.

When Poe was 26, he obtained a license to marry his 13-year-old cousin. The writer adored his wife during their 11 years of marriage. In 1841, he published *Murders in the Rue Morgue*, the first modern detective story. The following year he wrote *The Pit and the Pendulum* and *The Masque of the Red Death*. Poe was becoming more popular and the couple resided in Manhattan.

When Virginia contracted tuberculosis in 1846, Poe moved his wife to the cottage in the Bronx believing the air would be better. However, she succumbed to the disease and died in 1847. Near the bed where she died is Poe's original rocking chair. The cottage is also where Poe wrote some of his most important and best-known works including *Annabel Lee* and *The Bells*, both of which were published posthumously. Poe's life didn't continue much past the death of Virginia. He died in Baltimore in 1849.

The cottage was sold to New York City in 1913 and turned into a museum run by the Bronx County Historical Society. Virginia's bed is on the second floor accessible by a staircase. When in the house use your own phone to access the Poe Cottage Audio Tour at +1 (718)971-2156.

**Address** Grand Concourse and East Kingsbridge Road, Bronx, NY 10458, +1 (718)881-8900, www.bronxhistoricalsociety.org/poe-cottage, education@bronxhistoricalsociety.org | **Getting there** Subway to Kingsbridge Road (B, D train) | **Hours** Thu & Fri 10am–3pm, Sat 10am–4pm, Sun 1–5pm | **Tip** From June through November, the GrowNYC Poe Park Greenmarket brings fresh, local produce to the underserved neighborhood each Tuesday. Stop by for fresh fruits and vegetables (East 192nd Street, Bronx, NY 10451, www.grownyc.org/greenmarket/bronx/poe-park).

# 105 __ Wallworks New York

*Bridging the gap from graffiti world to art scene*

This contemporary art gallery in Mott Haven is the brainchild of graffiti pioneer John Matos (aka CRASH of TATS Cru) and entrepreneur Robert Kantor. It showcases new art from emerging and established artists in a gallery setting on par with Soho. Wallworks opened in 2014 and quickly became a popular destination in the neighborhood, with opening nights drawing enthusiastic crowds of artists, old friends from the neighborhood, and art fans from all over. The photography and graffiti exhibitions are memorable, but the real draw is attracting young people from the area and exposing them to a world-class art gallery.

"With the space, we wanted to make it very accessible where anyone can just come in and feel it's OK," Matos said. "Because growing up in that area of the South Bronx, most of us didn't go to galleries or museums unless it was school trips. So we wanted to have a place where people can feel OK to come in and look at stuff. To start a dialog and get their creative juices flowing."

Matos is a globetrotting graffiti artist and he leverages those trips to spread the word about the gallery. "Some of the artists we have shown I met them in Europe," Matos says. "So I can say, hey, we have this little place in the Bronx if you ever want to come and do something."

Wallworks is constantly changing with a wide variety of styles and artists presenting at a dizzying pace. Matos wishes the space was larger to have bigger shows. "We have group shows of local artists, some who've never shown before. We average between eight and ten shows a year, which is a lot of shows. But there are so many different artists out there. We're already four years in and we've done 40 or 50 exhibitions. We just call artists and friends up. Or artists come up to us during exhibitions and say hey, we know your work, we talk, and then boom, we're showing their work."

Address 39 Bruckner Boulevard, Bronx, NY 10454, +1 (917)825-9342, www.wallworksny.com, wallworksny@gmail.com | Getting there Subway to Third Avenue–138th Street (6 train) | Hours Check website for exhibition schedule | Tip Canal Place four blocks south served as a canal for the J. L. Mott Iron Works circa 1830s. It pushed nearly a mile inland to link iron factories to the Harlem River. In 1896, the board of health called for its closure. The canal was filled in and is today Canal Place and Canal Street (Canal Place, Bronx, NY 10451).

# 106___Water Lily & Lotus Pools

*The hot spot for horticulture fans at the NYBG*

Right in the middle of the Bronx is a place steeped in tradition, devoted fans, and faithful members with each new season. Passionate followers enter a magnificent steel structure to see newcomers and veterans at the New York Botanical Garden. Whether you were dragged here on a school field trip, you came here for a romantic stroll, or you needed a break from the stresses of everyday life, the NYBG will give you respite. It has been a beloved landmark since Grover Cleveland was in office and fire engines were pulled by horses.

Founded by a Columbia University botany professor in 1891, the NYBG opened to the public nine years later. The gardens cover 250 acres, with 12,000 live specimens and 5.8 million dried ones. NYBG owns a 50-acre, old growth forest, and the largest intact in the city. This is the closest you will get to experience what New York was like when explorers discovered it. The 19th century is everywhere in the gardens. Its most famous landmark, the glass-and-steel Enid A. Haupt Conservatory, covers one acre and has 17,000 panes of glass.

The water lilies and lotuses that grace the courtyard pools outside the conservatory are a wonder to behold. Floating green leaves, like platters, skim the surface, and the exquisite flowers bloom in extraordinary colors – hot pink, blue, lavender, yellow, white. If you are seeking a place to meditate, here it is. Held sacred by Buddhists for thousands of years, these aquatic plants mesmerize New Yorkers every summer. You'll want to spend some time just being here.

And then go visit the other sites. The landscaped area and rock garden is not to be missed. Spring is breathtaking, and the landscape is especially beautiful in the winter. Enjoy the numerous pieces of outdoor art and sculptures as well. NYBG staff are experts and can give you great tips and trivia about the flora in their care.

Address 2900 Southern Boulevard, Bronx, NY 10458, +1 (718)817-8700, www.nybg.org |
Getting there Metro-North to Botanical Garden (Harlem Line), or subway to Bedford
Park Boulevard (2, 4, B, D train), then transfer to bus Bx26 east to the Garden's Mosholu
entrance | Hours Daily 10am–6pm, check website for seasonal closings | Tip The biggest
event of the year at the NYBG is the Holiday Train Show. Miniature New York landmarks
and model trains draw huge crowds to this annual tradition (www.nybg.org/event/
holiday-train-show).

# 107__Wave Hill

*Nature at your fingertips*

There are only two Riverdale mansions open to the public, and they are both treasures of Wave Hill. Twenty-eight acres of gardens and sublime views of the Hudson River and New Jersey Palisades will draw you to this oasis. Cultivated gardens, woodlands, flower beds, and pathways surround a beautiful 1843 stone mansion and handsome 1920s estate house. Since the 1960s, the city has owned the property, and today Wave Hill offers tours and programming for visitors.

The 1840s mansion at the north end has been expanded and altered many times. Over the years, scores of wealthy residents and associates have visited Wave Hill, including Mark Twain, Charles Darwin, Theodore Roosevelt, and William Makepeace Thackeray. Millionaire George Walbridge Perkins owned Wave Hill during the Jazz Age and built a second mansion of red brick called Glyndor II in the Georgian style. Today, it houses an art gallery.

However, the real draw for visitors to Wave Hill isn't just mansions but the fabulous outdoor spaces. The botanical gardens, cultivated outdoor spaces, and horticultural exhibitions are among the finest in the city. The grounds appear to be trimmed by barbers and there are paths and walkways throughout. Take the wooded path in the back of the property for a nature walk that is only disturbed by the sounds of the Hudson Line rail cars many yards away. The many fine gardens include the Elliptical Garden with its formal design of native plant species, the cedar fence and arbors of the symmetric Flower Garden, and the Rossbach Monocot Garden with its amaryllis, lilies, orchids, grasses, and other members of the monocot plant group.

Wave Hill also features year-round public arts and event programming of all types, and it's popular with school groups and summer camps. A café provides healthy choices, with some of the edibles coming right from Wave Hill's own gardens.

Address 675 West 252nd Street, Bronx, NY 10471, +1 (718)549-3200, www.wavehill.org | Getting there Subway to 242nd Street (1 train) and take shuttle, or Metro-North to Riverdale and take shuttle | Hours Tue–Sun 9am–4:30pm, Mar 15–Oct 31 until 5:30pm | Tip Afternoon tea in the Wave Hill Café is offered at different times of the year. Green, black, and herbal whole-leaf teas are served with scones, tea sandwiches, and bite-sized desserts (675 West 249th Street, Bronx, NY 10471, www.wavehill.org/cafe).

# 108 West Farms Rapids

*Rushing water is a treat to see*

The only freshwater river in New York City is the Bronx River, which stretches 23 miles across the region. At one point, there are beautiful rapids to explore as the blue water rushes past the area. The rapids appear between 174th and 180th streets, known as the West Farms Rapids.

The Bronx River flows from northern Westchester to Hunts Point in the South Bronx, where it meets the East River. From the colonial era into the early 20th century, the Bronx River was an important part of commerce in the region. At one time, more than a dozen mills lined the banks and used the current to power the machinery of the Industrial Age. For several decades, the river was an open sewer. The city purchased the land around the river in the late 19th century, protecting it as a nature preserve. Generations of polluters dumped everything from old tires to refrigerators into the river. It was an eyesore and the community spoke up to clean it and rejuvenate the region. In the 1970s, the Bronx River Restoration Project launched what would become a 40-year campaign to make the area beautiful again. Today, it's one of the most bucolic spots in the borough.

The West Farms Rapids are located between the Bronx Zoo and Starlight Park and are composed of a tight series of rapids with a pathway alongside. At one time the pathway was a city road but it has since closed. A multi-year project by the New York City Department of Parks and Recreation to develop the parks along the riverbanks is underway. The Bronx River Alliance hosts volunteer days to clean up the park, activities on the water, and education about the natural resources. West Farms Rapids is busy in the spring and summer, and a visit to the rapids is a trip back in time to the colonial era. If you tune out the parkway and subway sounds, it's a peaceful time in a naturally beautiful setting.

Address Bronx River between East 180th Street and East Tremont Avenue, www.nycgovparks.org/parks/west-farms-rapids | Getting there Subway to 180th Street (2, 5 train) | Hours Daily 6–1am | Tip The 182nd Street Dam is at the border of River Park and the Bronx Zoo. A fish ladder passage was added in 2014 to allow ale fish to swim upriver to spawn (Bronx Park South and Boston Road, Bronx, NY 10460).

# 109 _ Wilson's Armistice Terms

*This Gilded Age mansion was a standby White House*

There are a lot of twists and turns in Riverdale, so walking around the streets on foot is the best way to admire the beautiful homes and scenery in this corner of the Bronx. One of these homes does not have a historic landmark plaque, but it played an important role in the end of World War I.

Cleveland Hoadley Dodge (1860–1926) was a copper baron and philanthropist. He was a proud graduate of Princeton. It was Dodge who put his classmate, New Jersey Gov. Woodrow Wilson, into the president's chair of Princeton and was later a White House confidant when Wilson became president of the United States in 1916. On October 12, 1918, Dodge was with Wilson in New York reviewing a Liberty Bond parade, as American forces in France were in the midst of the Meuse-Argonne campaign, the bloodiest era of the war for the US An urgent telegram from Imperial Germany was handed to the president at the parade, asking for Wilson's peace terms.

Dodge took Wilson back to his home in Riverdale to discuss what to do next. It was in the home's library that Wilson penned a reply to the Germans, dictating the US peace terms. Wilson's response was that the US would only negotiate with a democratic Germany, not an imperial state with a military dictatorship. Every day the war continued was costing thousands of lives. The response was sent. Less than a month later, on November 11, the armistice was signed.

The orange brick neo-Georgian mansion on Dodgewood Road was built for Dodge in the 1880s. He called it Naumkeag, the Native American name for Salem, Massachusetts. Naumkeag is a gracious, brick neo-Georgian with impressive rounded portico around the front entrance. As large as the house appears, it once was bigger: the side wings were detached, moved away from the home, and are now separate houses on Dodgewood Road. The mansion next door, called Greystone, was also a Dodge property.